RESCUING

THE

DEVOURED

The Church's Need
For a New Normal

Making Mango Trees

David A. Rusco

Table of Contents

Acknowledgments.. 5

Introduction.. 7

Chapter 1 A Devoured Christian............................. 15

Chapter 2 Demons and Tumbleweeds.......................... 21

Chapter 3 Who Are You In Christ?.......................... 27

Chapter 4 Demonic Opposition.............................. 37

Chapter 5 What Jesus Did To The Opposition......... 45

Chapter 6 Deliverance meeting outline.................. 51

Chapter 7 Normal Deliverance Meeting.................. 55

Chapter 8 Confronting Demons............................. 81

Chapter 9 Other Deliverance Ministry Issues......... 97

Chapter 10 Healing/Prayer Ministry....................... 103

End Notes... 119

Ministry Release Form...................................... 121

Acknowledgments

I would like to acknowledge and thank several people who have allowed this deliverance ministry to begin and continue to this day.

First of all, I thank my wife Donna, who has given up many hours as I have ministered to others during these last 35 years.

Second, to Atascadero Bible Church pastors E.B. Claud and Tom Ferrell, for allowing me to begin and continue this deliverance ministry. I thank Tom for allowing me to use his office, many times after hours.

Third, I want to thank my fellow pastors, Darren Rusco and Mark Wheeler, here at Paso Robles Bible Church, for allowing me more time to expand this ministry.

I also want to thank my good friends Steve Adams and Dee Dee Bernal for proof reading and trying to correct all my punctuation and English errors.

Last, but not least, I thank Jesus for allowing me the privilege of meeting and working with hundreds of His saints and giving me the joy of seeing them find freedom from the devourer.

Introduction

Be of sober spirit, be on the alert. Your adversary, the devil,
prowls around like a roaring lion, seeking someone to devour.
1 Peter 5:8

The word *devour* in 1 Peter 5:8 means to drink down, swallow down, destroy. This is what the devil wants to do to every believer. It's the ultimate scheme of the devil. Much of the church has been ignorant of the devil's schemes. We simply do not understand the working of the devil's angels today. We have been blinded to what demons are doing to many Christian men, women and children. It's time to embrace the authority we have in Christ. It's time we begin to help our brothers and sisters out of these demonic schemes and their devastating results. The Church needs to be set free. Today's church needs a new normal.

When I became a believer in 1974, I was 24 years old. I did not grow up in a Christian home. I never attended a church. When God saved me I was like an empty vessel. More accurately, I was like a sponge. I soaked up Biblical truths and began memorizing God's Word. I eventually began teaching children and then adults. It wasn't long before the church asked me to be an elder. I felt I was much too young to be an elder, both spiritually and physically, but I said "yes" and accepted the position.

This was during the 1970's. The Jesus movement was happening in Southern California. New praise and worship music made its way up the coast to central California where I lived, and I began leading our congregation as a worship leader. I was an elder, teacher and worship leader in my church. It was a wonderful time for my wife and me and our two small children.

But there was an area in my life that I just could not get a handle on. I was crying out to God for help. One day I was talking with an older Christian man about this - and he told me my issue was usually demonic. Demonic??? That shocked me. I totally discounted that. I was a Christian. I was taught demons could not do these things to Christians. After all, the Holy Spirit resided in me. My friend said, "Dave, if that's what you've been taught, you better read your Bible again." I was not ready to concede that my problem could be demonically empowered.

Sometime later our church hosted a leadership conference. Our pastor invited Dr. Ed Murphy[1], one of his seminary professors, to speak to the leaders of our church. I didn't know it, but Dr. Murphy also had a ministry in spiritual warfare. As he was speaking to us, from time to time, he would say something regarding spiritual warfare that especially caught my attention.

I went up and spoke to him after one of our sessions. He told me he was involved in sending missionaries to other cultures. Many of them were coming back to the United States chewed up, devoured by the devil. They hadn't been properly prepared. To correct this issue he developed a series of teaching tapes on spiritual warfare for their missionaries. He had one set of these tapes with him and asked me if I wanted it. "Yes!"

In those days I worked for a pest control company and I would listen to the tapes during my drive time between work sites. After listening to his biblical teaching and his many personal testimonies, I soon had no doubt that demons could do these kinds of things to believers.

In one of the tapes he began to use his authority and commanded certain demons to leave the one who was listening to the tapes. He was commanding them to leave me as I was driving down the freeway! I was agreeing with him. I was saying, "Yes! Go. Leave."

I didn't notice anything different at first. I just kept driving. But later that day I began to notice a sensitivity to anything dark or sinful. I would look at a billboard in passing and feel repulsed. I would watch TV and again feel repulsed by many things I saw. That was new. It just had not been my experience prior to this event.

I could hardly believe what had happened. The demonic foothold was completely gone from my life. I noticed that the temptation might be there occasionally, but I could easily resist it and just say no. There was a huge difference in my life and even in my marriage. I thought, "If this could happen to and for me it could happen to and for any other believer."

I brought this baggage into my Christian life and no one confiscated it when I became saved. It was in my life both before and after I became a believer in Jesus Christ. I was a normal Christian man. I was an Elder and worship leader in my church. No one would have ever known that this foothold sin issue existed within my life.

The Bible says, *"Submit therefore to God. Resist the devil and he will flee from you" (James 4:7).* I thought I had submitted myself to God previously. But I never resisted the devil. I wasn't taught to. It wasn't part of the church's vocabulary or practice. I was taught that submitting myself actually was resisting the devil. Not true. Therefore, the devil or demons never fled from me...not until a man named Ed Murphy helped me to resist them.

For 35 years now I have been helping other believers do the same thing. I have met with and helped hundreds of Christian men, women and children to become free from demonic devouring or footholds in their lives.

This book is written to guide you to help others find that same freedom. Allow me to repeat myself. I believe the church has been ignorant of the devil's schemes. Most church leaders and believers simply do not understand what demons can do to Christian men, women and children.[2] It's time we begin to help our brothers and sisters out of these demonic footholds. The church needs a new normal. It needs to be set free.

Sadly, many of our friends, family and other dear believers live their Christian lives without ever dealing with the devil who may be literally devouring them in varying degrees. In many cases the world and the church have given names to the symptoms they are experiencing, names such as depression, ADHD, chronic fatigue syndrome, and migraine headaches. The symptoms are real. The question then is what causes the symptoms? Yes, it can be just a physical issue. But why are we not looking for the possibility of a spiritual cause? In many cases believers live with the world's names and the world's treatments for these symptoms. Many believers that come to me have tried the world's treatments first. But if the cause is spiritual, they are in great need of biblical truth and spiritual help to remove footholds.

I believe these footholds are pervasive in the church today. These demons are tempting, accusing, deceiving and lying to unsuspecting saints. In every case where they've gained a foothold, they're causing emotional issues and in some cases causing physical issues in their lives.

Too many husbands and wives are struggling to survive conflicts and deceptions through worldly means, not knowing there are evil spirits trying to take their marriage out. They don't understand the real root of their problem or what to do about it.

All of our friends in the church today are struggling against *spiritual forces of wickedness (Eph. 6:12)* but too many are ignorant of what's actually going on. Too many of our friends are being hit by fiery arrows or experiencing what the Scriptures refer to as devouring (1 Peter 5:8). It's time we begin to help our brothers and sisters out of these demonic footholds (devouring) and set the church free.

Over the years we have accepted this state of the church as "normal." Husbands are leaving their wives and believers are bound by pornography and X-rated minds. Others are battling anger and forgiveness issues. Others are being hit with fear, panic, worry and depression. When we gather on Sunday morning no one ever knows what's happening in our minds. Everyone comes with a smile and nice clothes. But the flaming arrows of the evil one are hitting our brothers and sisters and even they are not aware of what's really happening. We seem to be like frogs in a pan of water which is slowly heating – oblivious to what is happening until we find ourselves cooked and devoured.

Too many saints of God are not wielding the sword of the Spirit or lifting up the shield of faith to stop these attacks (Eph. 6:16). We have accepted this as "normal", but we should not. There are too many without joy, without peace, without freedom. Pastors are burdened down trying to help these dear saints. Too many pastors themselves are being devoured to varying degrees. Often these dear pastors can't help devoured saints so they refer them to doctors and psychologists.

The plant is drooping. The leaves are wilting. Seldom can you heal the plant by working on the leaves. You must go to the root. When the root problems are gone the plant flourishes. The leaves are then healthy. The root problems are often demonic. Remove the footholds and teach them how to be alert and the plant flourishes.

One day a Christian man I'll call John phoned me. There was an area in John's life, written of in the lusts of the flesh (Galatians 5), that he had no victory over – pornography and an X-rated mind. He wanted to know if the intensity of this could be demonically empowered. I told him, "Let's meet and we'll find out." When John and I met I led him through a simple process. I helped him submit himself to God. I helped him resist the devil and the devil fled from him (James 4:7). The demonic foothold gained in his past was removed. The power of that foothold was gone from his life. The bondage of pornography and fantasy was over. The Lord brought a great healing. Now, many years later, his freedom continues to this day.

What I'm about to teach you is not rocket science. But it has the potential to help countless numbers of believers in our churches today. There needs to be a new normal in the church and this is one of the areas of greatest need. Most of the dear brothers and sisters I have met with have received healing and deliverance from the Lord. The need for this ministry appears to be greater today than ever before. And the lack of this ministry within the local church is glaring, especially when the need is so great.

I'm writing this book because of a conversation I recently had with my son Darren. He asked me, "Dad, do you know what the fruit of a mango tree is?" With raised eyebrows and a question mark in my eyes, I said, "No. Could it be mangos?" He said, "Other mango trees." Then he asked, "Who's going to continue this ministry when you're gone?" The point he was making is this: I'm 65 years old. I'm a single mango tree and I need to be producing other mango trees. I need to multiply myself and help others to bring healing and deliverance to their friends and others in the body of Christ. Therefore, this book is designed to create mango trees. I desire to teach you. I desire to help you and activate you to help your friends who need to be set free from footholds that plague them.

I'm not going to spend much time trying to convince you of the need for this ministry. If you're reading this book you most likely already see it. Nor will I spend much time trying to convince you, biblically, what demons can do to Christians. You have a pretty good idea already. That's not my purpose here. There are many other books that accomplish that purpose[3]. But I will help you bring healing to your Christian friends who are being devoured by the devil (1 Peter 5:8) and who are being hit by flaming arrows (Eph. 6:16). I will help you teach your friends how to lift up the shield of faith and STOP the flaming arrows of the evil one from hitting them. If I succeed in this goal, then you must remember that you are also a mango tree and among your duties is to create new mango trees. Will you join me in rescuing the devoured?

Chapter One

A Devoured Christian

When I say devoured, what comes to your mind? Eaten? Chewed up and swallowed down? It's not a pleasant term. Christians are warned in Scripture to be alert and not allow the devil (demons) to devour them. Sadly, often this alertness doesn't happen.

> *1 Peter 5:8*
>
> *8 Be of sober spirit, be on the alert. Your adversary, the devil, prowls around like a roaring lion, seeking someone to devour.*
>
> *9 But resist him, firm in your faith...*

Let me repeat the meaning of the word *devour*. It means to drink down, swallow, destroy[4]. Peter, remember, is writing to believers. In the first century these Christians were experiencing much tribulation and suffering. It would have been easy for them to faint under the demonic lie that no one else had as much trouble as they did, or that God's love had left them. They needed to know that the same suffering was also happening to other brothers and sisters throughout the world. These believers were to resist the devil's lies with scriptural truth, just as Jesus did. Devouring comes as a result of believing the devil's lies. So from this point forward when I use the term devour or devouring, I'm referring to the Christian believing lies from the world, the flesh and the demons. Demonic lies are temptations, accusations and deceptions spoken into the minds of believers. Often they cannot distinguish between their own thoughts and demonic thoughts and temptations.

What can happen to a believer who is being devoured? Here's an example from my ministry. One day a man called the church around 10:30 am. Our office manager answered the phone call. Jim[5] wanted to talk to me. The office manager told me he didn't sound very good. I could tell that was true when I began to listen to him. I found out this was a man in his 50's and a believer who went to a church in another city. He was very depressed, downtrodden and defeated. I asked if he could come to see me that same day at one o-clock.

When he arrived we met in a quiet, private room where there's no foot traffic and no phones. He told me he was a believer and has served in his church for 30 years. As we talked I learned he struggled with anger, bitterness, forgiveness and depression. He told me he has experienced depression much of his life. This middle-aged man was being devoured by the devil, or more specifically, demons. We met three times within two weeks. We removed several spirits that had footholds in his life. He'd been listening to these spirits for most of his life. He couldn't discern that the emotions and thoughts in his mind were not his, but the demons. He told me at the beginning of our second meeting the depression left and that he felt better than he ever has. Today his mind and emotions are clear. His passion for Jesus is greater than ever. I could tell this kind of story hundreds of times.

When our brothers and sisters are struggling with any of the lusts (or deeds) of the flesh (Galatians 5:19-21), it very well could be empowered by demons. Demons empower the following list in our lives. Let's spend a little time here in Galatians 5:

Galatians 5:19-21

19 Now the deeds of the flesh are evident, which are: immorality, impurity, sensuality (sexual sins) *20 idolatry, sorcery,* (spiritual sins) *enmities, strife, jealousy, outbursts of anger, disputes, dissensions, factions, 21 envying, drunkenness, carousing, and things like these* (social sins).

We will all struggle with various areas of the flesh. God has not removed the flesh from us on this earth. But when this struggle seems to dominate the believer, when we compulsively sin in one or more of these areas, it may be that a demonic foothold is there empowering the flesh. So being devoured or being hit with flaming arrows may be occurring when a believer is compulsively yielding to one or more of these areas.

The first three are in the moral realm: *Immorality, impurity, sensuality.* This covers all sexual sin, including the fantasy-thinking realm. If a believer is struggling with or compulsively yielding to pornography, masturbation, or sexual fantasy, demons are usually empowering this behavior. Devouring is taking place. They will need help in removing these strongholds.

The next two are spiritual sins: *idolatry, sorcery.* If someone claims to be a Christian and yet their lives are entrenched in earthly things, devouring may be taking place. Another possibility could be they are not saved. If anything takes first place in our lives other than Jesus, *idolatry* is the issue. The American dream is a powerful draw to some of our Christian friends. Idolatry is common in the life of those outside of Christ and much more common within the church than most of us realize.

Next is *sorcery.* How can this lust of the flesh manifest in a believers life? A desire for more of God's power in our lives is not a wrong desire. But caution and discernment is needed. The demons often masquerade as angels of light. They even can deceive believers into thinking their demonic power is the Holy Spirit's power.

Eve was hearing words she thought came from the Holy Spirit. She wisely wanted to test the spirit but felt she needed help. She called me and we met together with my wife. After prayer, I said, "I want the spirit that has been speaking to Eve to come before me now. The Bible tells us to test the spirits to see whether they are from God or not." I asked this spirit the following questions. "Has Jesus Christ come in the flesh?" "Is Jesus Christ Lord?" "Is Jesus the creator of all things." That spirit spoke into the mind of Eve and answered all my questions correctly. But I believed this was an evil, religious spirit and not the Holy Spirit. I've never had the Holy Spirit answer questions like that. The fact that he was answering my questions as demons do, raised red flags before me. How could I expose him? He answered my questions correctly. Finally I asked the spirit, "Do you understand that God created the Lake of fire for the devil and his angels and they will be confined there forever?" That spirit screamed out in her mind the word, "No!" Her eyes were wide open like quarters. We then knew the truth concerning this spirit. This was not the Holy Spirit, but rather a deceiving spirit who came to her as a messenger of light. The power manifesting in her life was from the devil, not from God. With her full approval I had her renounce the work of this spirit in her life. She also asked God to forgive her. Then I commanded that spirit to leave and release her. She was freed from that lying, deceiving spirit.

The third group are social sins: *enmities, strife, jealousy, outbursts of anger, disputes, dissensions, factions, envying, drunkenness, carousing, and things like these.* Whenever these things are happening between Christian people in the church, there are often demons at the root of them. James warns us:

> *James 3:14-16*
> *14 But if you have bitter jealousy and selfish ambition in your heart, do not be arrogant and so lie against the truth. 15 This wisdom is not that which comes down from above, but is earthly, natural, demonic. 16 For where jealousy and selfish ambition exist, there is disorder and every evil thing.*

In some cases the demons have access through footholds in this third group. They can devour you, your friends and your church, causing strife, division and disorder. Often times believers with footholds here have strife and disorder in their homes. You can help your friends. They may need prayer, deliverance and healing.

Next, allow me next to explain the two locations from which demons operate.

Chapter Two

Demons and Tumbleweeds

When I walked out of my office last week I noticed a large brown tumbleweed lodged against the fence which surrounds our grass playground area at church. I asked pastor Darren, he's also my son, "Where did that tumbleweed come from? I wonder how it got here?" The only answer is that it blew in the wind. The word "spirit," referring to an evil spirit, is the Greek word *pneuma,* the word for wind. Allow me to explain the two locations from which demons operate.

First: They're everywhere in the wind or the air space. They're tempting, accusing and deceiving (TAD) people. We can't see them, but I believe they are often next to us speaking into our minds. You've probably walked into a store or a place where you could feel the presence of demons. It just felt dark, heavy and evil there. That's because it, most likely, was.

One day I was doing a termite inspection on a vacant, old three story Victorian house. This was one of my many previous jobs before God called me to be a pastor/teacher. After we arrived at the house, the realtor told me this house had the reputation of being haunted. "Great!" I thought to myself. But I knew this information only meant that demons were still there from past tenants and activities that had occurred in that house. Yes, as I was walking through this huge, three story, old house and basement, I actually felt demons there. As I walked through the attic to an outside ledge walkway I heard strange noises. I just told them to be quiet. They knew who I was, and they knew that I knew who they were. I had no fear. The Holy Spirit in me is greater than they who are in the world.

The house had termites, so I sent a fumigation company to the house to measure it for a cost estimate to cover the house with tarps to kill the termites. Later I received a call from the head man on the fumigation crew. He told me they weren't going to bid on that job. I asked why. He said when he went through the attic to the second story walkway something tried to push him off the roof. He was terrified. He ran away from that house as fast as his feet would take him and said, "I'm never going back there!" This man was not a believer and didn't understand the unseen demonic realm. But they never touched me the two days I was there, even though I felt their presence. I also know they felt my presence. So demons are everywhere. They are in the air space. That's why I ask God to station His angels at my house, especially when we sleep. I don't want the enemy there when my wife and I are asleep...or awake.

Here's what they can do from the air space. Since we can't see them, they often will speak into our minds. Their speaking comes in the form of thoughts. Normally these thoughts come in the first person singular as if you are thinking the thoughts. I'll have thoughts like, "I'm not really a pastor." "I can't teach people." "I can't write this book." "I'm too old to be relevant." "Who do I think I am?" "I need to quit." If the demons can get you to believe these kinds of thoughts, that their thoughts or lies are actually your own thoughts, they have won a great victory in your life. If they deceive you into thinking their temptations, accusations and deceptive thoughts are actually your own thoughts, eventually they can get you to act upon them.

The Bible tells us to take every thought captive in obedience to Christ (2 Cor. 10:3-5). In other words, don't let those thoughts run free in our minds. Don't dwell on those lies. Resist them firm in your faith. *Set your mind on things above, not on things that are on earth (Col. 3:2)*...judge every thought. So the first location from which demons operate is the air space. They are just out there and can actually be near us from time to time.

But they are not content to just be around us speaking (TAD) temptation, accusation and deceptive thoughts into our minds.

The second location demons operate from is a place, a foothold in the life of a believer. From this foothold they gain more power in the believers mind, emotions and body.

Jim had several demons who had gained a foothold in his life. When they were removed, their power was significantly reduced in his mind, emotions and body. Our ministry is to remove footholds. We then teach men and women of God how to submit to God and resist the devil. We teach them how to take every thought captive (2 Cor. 10:5). My desire is to eliminate footholds and any further possibility of footholds being gained by the demons.

> *Ephesians 4:26-27*
> *Be angry, and yet do not sin; do not let the sun go down*
> *on your anger 27 and do not give the devil an*
> *opportunity (foothold, place).*

The Greek word *opportunity* literally means *a place*. Demons can take a place in a believer's life. From this location they have more power in that life (mind, emotions, body). In this verse the sin of not dealing with anger can open a door for demons into the believer's life. Demons devour from having footholds in our lives. They have great patience in gaining and keeping their footholds in the lives of believers.

Oftentimes believers cannot distinguish between demonic thoughts and their own thoughts. They've been listening to demonic thoughts for so long they can't distinguish them. They will need our help to recognize and out-truth the demonic lies.

Early in this ministry I was talking to a lady named

Jessica. Jessica was experiencing many emotional difficulties. She wanted to know if this could be demonically empowered. I said, "Let's find out." As I listen to people's stories I look for doors that the enemy may have taken. We can close those doors, stop the devouring, remove footholds and bring healing. Jessica told me her story. She had been sexually abused by her father through her childhood. This was certainly a door. Her father was struggling with demonic footholds in his own life. Through sexual sin and abuse, demons can gain a foothold in a victims life and then they will patiently devour.

Jessica was now a middle-aged adult. Her emotions and thoughts were taking her out. She was depressed, angry and confused. She needed help. When she came to see me I first led her through *The Steps To Freedom*.[6] These are seven steps or possible doorways for the enemy to gain a foothold into our lives. Step 3 is the doorway of Bitterness verses Forgiveness. She read (prayed) a prayer asking the Lord to reveal to her all the people she hadn't forgiven in order that she may do so. She wrote down many names on the paper I gave her. These were people that she held anger toward, bitterness or a lack of forgiveness. Her father was the first name on her list. She began by forgiving everyone on her list except her father. She could not forgive him. I knew she had to for her healing and deliverance to take place.

I explained to her what forgiveness was and what it wasn't. Forgiveness is an act of obedience. It's not based upon our emotion. We're commanded to forgive each other. I told her God did not create us to live with anger, bitterness, hatred and unforgiveness. We weren't made to keep others on "our" hook. That only hurts us. I told her, "You're dad is on God's hook. God said, 'Vengeance is mine, I will repay.'" Again I said, "Jessica, let your father off your hook. Forgive him. He's on the right hook, God's." I told her that forgiving her father does not condone what he did. I know of nothing worse than to treat your own daughter like that. I told her forgiving is not forgetting what he did. After quite some time she finally told me, "Ok Dave, I'll forgive my dad for what he did to me, but I don't feel it. It's just because of obedience to Jesus. I do this by faith."

I helped her construct her prayer. But she prayed, "Lord, help me to forgive my dad..." I interrupted her, "Can I stop you here? Don't say, 'Help me to forgive.' But rather, 'I forgive my dad.' 'Forgive him.'" She started over with much difficulty. "Lord, ...I forgive my dad for abusing me all those years." She finally got those words out to God. God heard her statement of obedient faith. He's always pleased with our faith and obedience. A miracle took place just at that moment. She had a continual smile on her face. I asked her, "Jessica, what's going on?" She told me a weight just lifted. She told me it was as if it lifted off her shoulders. A healing took place at that very moment. We easily removed several foothold enemies of the Lord Jesus Christ. It was a wonderful time of victory and healing. Three days later she called and said, "Dave, you're not going to believe what has happened to me." I asked, "What, Jessica?" She told me, "I actually now feel forgiveness toward my dad." That was a great victory and healing.

Forgiveness doesn't mean it condones the sins of others, but it does stop others from continuing to torment your soul with memories of some past experience. Nor does forgiveness necessarily mean we forget. It doesn't mean Jessica would take her children to her dad for him to watch the kids. Jessica was healed and her spiritual growth now continues with a greater passion for a miraculous God.

All of our brothers and sisters are struggling with the world, the flesh, and the devil and many are in various stages of being devoured. I believe this is a common thing in all our churches. Our job is to love and help each other and not to overlook the possibility of footholds in our friend's lives.

Here are some of the other areas of devouring that I have helped my friends out of by removing footholds.

Depression, fear, panic, anger, rage, hatred, unforgiveness, thoughts of suicide, confusion, inability to make decisions, pride, control, self-mutilation, nightmares, immorality, pornography, lust, sexual fantasy, masturbation, religious spirits, condemning thoughts, diverting thoughts, stealing, criticism, alcohol, drugs, tobacco, compulsive addictive behavior, eating disorders and curses. Also physical issues such as migraine headaches, chronic fatigue, irritable bowel syndrome, and lactose intolerance. These and many other physical problems have been healed by removing footholds.

Often someone's parents and/or grandparents will have struggled with these same demonic issues. Footholds from prior generations can enter the life of a baby, even at birth. Then, as the child grows, demonic issues can become more apparent. The child will experience the same oppression its parents or grandparents struggled with. The world understands this reality, but not its underlying cause. Through biblical deliverance ministry, these doors can be closed and demonic footholds removed. We will discuss this later in more depth.

My brothers and sisters, being devoured by the devil is a very serious thing. The wonderful truth is you can help others who are being devoured. Let me make you into a mango tree. Are you ready? First you need to know who you are in Christ. In the following chapter we will look at what the Bible has to say concerning who you really are as a believer in Jesus Christ, especially as it relates to confronting the demonic realm.

Chapter Three

Who Are You In Christ?

It is very important that you to know who you are in Christ. You must have a firm grasp of this truth when helping your friends and fellow believers out of demonic footholds and various levels of devouring.

Often the demons try to elevate their power over me. They will tell me they are stronger than I am or they have more power than I do. Usually they talk to me by speaking into the mind of the one I'm helping. It comes to him or her in the form of thoughts. The person then relays those thoughts to me verbally. Demons representing themselves as stronger than me is a lie. They are very good at lying. That's their nature. They've been doing it for thousands of years. Although they are angels and these angelic beings are older, more experienced and more powerful than any mere human being, that's not true for the Christian believer. We have their Creator, Jesus, living **in us**. If Christ is in us and Christ is for us, who can be against us (Rom. 8:31)?

Have you ever played poker? If you have, you know the other players often try to bluff you into thinking they have a better hand than you have. Demons do the very same thing. But we know the truth in God's Word. They can never bluff me in this area. I know who I am in Christ. You and I have no need to bluff because we are holding the winning hand. We all need to know this truth.

We are holding a Royal Flush. The five cards you hold in your hand correspond to five critical truths.

Ace: The Holy Spirit in you is greater than the demons (spirits) who are in the world.

> *1 John 4:4*
> *You are from God, little children, and have overcome them; because greater is He who is in you than he who is in the world.*

King: You are united with Jesus and you are one spirit with Him.

> *1 Cor. 6:17*
> *But the one who joins himself to the Lord is one spirit with Him.*

Queen: Jesus in you is the head over all rule and authority (demons).

> *Col. 2:10*
> *And in Him you have been made complete, and He is the head over all rule and authority.*

Jack: You've been given authority over demons.

> *Luke 10:19*
> *Behold, I have given you authority to tread on serpents and scorpions, and over all the power of the enemy, and nothing will injure you.*

Ten: You will do the very same works that Jesus did.

> *John 14:12*
> *Truly, truly, I say to you, he who believes in Me, the works that I do, he will do also;*

Those five truths are like a Royal Flush in the game of Five-card Draw poker. Nothing can top it. You carry the winning hand, always. As I said earlier, the demons will sometimes challenge my authority by proclaiming they are more powerful than I am...that they have a better hand than I do. I know those are lies. I pull out the sword of the Spirit, which is the Word of God, and I quote a couple of these "Five Card" passages and those lies stop right there.

One afternoon I met with a dear Christian believer who I will call Earl. Earl owned his own business and for years was trapped into thinking as the world thinks. He sought for more money, more things and more prestige. Manipulation was his way of life. Anger and pride had very strong holds in his life. He actually used his anger for the manipulation of others. After listening to my teaching, one day He came to me. He wanted to know if the anger in his life was more than just him. I replied, "Let's meet and find out."

First, I took him through *the Steps to Freedom In Christ*. This will strengthen the believer. Afterward, in the confrontation stage, I wanted to know if there was a spirit called "Anger" that had a foothold in Earl's life. In just a short moment, a spirit called "Anger" was there. There is a process I follow in most cases to remove these spirits. But this spirit attempted to intimidate me. All of a sudden this man began to laugh. Not just a slight laughter, but a full-out belly laugh. I knew this was the spirit and not Earl and I knew what the spirit was trying to do... intimidate, bluff and divert me.

This was certainly an unusually powerful spirit. He took control of Earl's body and caused him to laugh at me. It wasn't Earl, it was the spirit. I looked into Earl's eyes and told the spirit, "You're not staying here. You are going to leave. I know it and you know it." The laughter kept coming. I continued using my authority and said, "You, spirit of anger, go right through that wall." I pointed to the exterior wall. "You release Earl's mind, now." Just at that point the laughter instantly stopped. It was either my command, or he knew this laughter wasn't working for him. I would not be distracted. Now the spirit was in danger of losing his foothold. So he tried another tactic. He then began to choke Earl. I told the spirit, "Leave this man of God alone. You... leave! Now! Release his emotions and his body. I command you in the name of Jesus to go. Leave our presence...right now! Get out of here!" The choking stopped and his body relaxed. "Earl, did that spirit leave?" I asked. "Yes", he answered, with a slight smile on his face. All Earl could say then was, "Wow." I explained to him that this is the process of deliverance. Many other spirits also lost their footholds on that afternoon.

Bluffing is what demons often do. They do not want to lose their foothold. Once I command their attention and they are answering my questions in submission to Christ's authority in me, I know it's just a matter of time before they are gone. I have authority from Jesus to remove demons. As a believer in Jesus you have that same authority. I will continue to explain this process as we progress.

Allow me to explain your position in Christ a different way. I've been an athlete most of my life. I love to watch replays on the sports channels or YouTube, especially golf. Of course, in this case, I already know the outcome of those golf matches. When I watch a sporting event that I already know the outcome of, it totally changes the experience of watching it. I already know who will win and what will happen.

I recently watched a replay of the 1988 World Series between the L.A. Dodgers and Oakland A's. This was the first game of the series. Kirk Gibson came to bat in the bottom of the 9th for the Dodgers. He had an injury to his leg and couldn't play. But, surprisingly, they sent him up to pinch hit in the bottom of the ninth even though he couldn't run. He limped to the batters box. I remember thinking as I was watching this game live on TV, why would Gibson be pinch hitting when he couldn't run? Plus, he was batting against Dennis Eckersley, one of the premier relief pitchers in the game. His chances did not look good.

But I already know the outcome. I'm not nervous or shaking my head wondering why he's pinch hitting. I already know what's going to happen. He's going hit a home run into the right field bleachers and win the game by the score of 5-4. I can still see him limping around the bases pumping his right arm in that victory lap to home plate. Knowing the outcome of the event before it happens changes everything. I'm watching from the vantage point of victory.

Christian friend, we already know the outcome. Jesus Christ has won the victory over anything the devil brings at you. This is the truth. It takes fear, anxiety and doubt out of the game for every believer who knows this truth. We're playing on God's team. We're playing for the One who has already won. It changes everything. It changes how you walk, talk and love. You walk in humble authority and great hope. That's not the "hope-so" kind of hope, it's the "know-so" kind of hope. You possess this God-given authority and you can use it to help bring freedom and healing to your brothers and sisters in Christ.

This is an area of ministry that is greatly needed in the body of Christ. Most churches will not address this need and it is affecting a great percentage of God's people. My prayer is that you continue in this book and step out in faith to help your brothers and sisters in Christ.

But a note of caution is due here. For this ever to be a ministry within your church, you must have the approval and support of the leaders of your church. This should be an issue of prayer. Sad to say, but many church leaders will not approve of this ministry. Some 35 years ago I began to schedule deliverance meetings with people at my church. I was not on staff at the time and I did not obtain prior permission from the leadership. Although I was an Elder, some others in leadership had a different view on this whole subject and they didn't agree with or understand my ministry.

My pastor asked if he could sit in on a few of my meetings. I told him, "Yes, anytime." He watched my ministry for a period of time and told me to keep going, although it was done quietly without much fanfare. I continued and saw many of my friends and others in the church community released from demonic activity.

Eventually, our church planted a daughter church in a nearby community with me as the founding pastor. Today, after about 13 years in the new church, this ministry is much more in the open. Presently I have several others also ministering with me in this arena. Together, we are now serving people from other churches as well. The need is great.

Let me ask you a question. What does every believer, new and old, need to become a disciple of Jesus? Among the many things needed, let me suggest a few. They will need baptism, teaching, filling with the Spirit, deliverance ministry, healing, blessing, and accountability. I consider this the "new normal" for the church. I include the deliverance ministry because many, if not most, who become saved in our day will need this ministry of deliverance.

Let's continue to explore who we are in Christ.

Ephesians 1:18-19

I pray that the eyes of your heart may be enlightened, so that you will know ... what is the surpassing greatness of His power toward us who believe.

The believers in Ephesus didn't realize the greatness of His power toward them. That's why Paul prayed for them to know it. There's more for us to "know" (experiential knowledge). Do you know the "surpassing greatness of His power toward you?" Paul prayed for these believers to experience more of the power already given to them in Christ. Certainly this power in our lives is the power that changes us into Christ's image. It's the power to be victorious and passionate in our walk for Christ. It would also include the power to *do*, not just to *be*. It even includes the power to bring healing into the lives of our brothers and sisters who are being hit with flaming arrows and being devoured by demons.

Paul writes this power can accomplish more than we can even imagine.

> *Ephesians 3:20-21*
> *20 Now to him who is able to do far more abundantly beyond all that we ask or think, according to the power that works within us, 21 to Him be the glory in the church and in Christ Jesus to all generations forever and ever. Amen.*

This power and authority is for everyone who believes in Jesus.

> *John 14:12*
> *Truly, truly, I say to you, he who believes in Me, the works that I do, he will do also; and greater works than these he will do; because I go to the Father.*

What happened when Jesus went to the Father? He sent the Holy Spirit and the Spirit's power and authority into the lives of every believer. The power of the Spirit would manifest in the believers life. They would do the very same things that Jesus did... *anyone who has faith in me will do what I have been doing.* That would include loving your neighbor, proclaiming the gospel of the kingdom, healing the sick and casting out demons. There's no time limit for these passages. Nowhere does it say these Words of God are applicable only for the first century church, but they are for everyone who believes in Jesus. The question is, how great is your faith to act upon this authority?

Have you seen commercials that advertise a huge looking hamburger, but when you buy one it looks nothing like the advertisement? I remember a commercial on TV years ago. An older lady buys a hamburger at a fast-food restaurant. She looks closely at it and then complains, "Where's the beef?" If Jesus said that anyone who has faith in Him would do what He had been doing, then my question is, "Where's the beef? Where's the faith?" Where's the confidence in the plain truth of Scripture?

> *James 5:14-15*
> *14 Is anyone among you sick? Then he must call for the elders of the church and they are to pray over him, anointing him with oil in the name of the Lord;*
> *15 and the prayer offered in faith will restore the one who is sick, and the Lord will raise him up.*

Some here at the church where I minister have been healed through the prayers of the elders, but even more through the prayer ministry of one another. One day in my home group one of our ladies came with a very swollen and painful hand. She had been kicked that afternoon by a cow while holding a shovel. The hoof split her finger open. Another of our ladies in our home group who was helping her that day said it was to the bone. She came with it all wrapped up. She was an older lady, but a cowgirl in every sense of the word and a new believer. She asked for prayer.

The ladies gathered around her and began praying for healing. They were careful touching her hand because of the pain. As they were silent, waiting over her after they had prayed, they asked how she was feeling. She said her hand was tingling. That seemed like a good sign, so they continued praying and waiting. After a short time they again asked her how she felt. She said the pain in her hand was now gone. All eyes were glued on her as she unwrapped her hand. You could sense the anticipation. The swelling was gone. The pain was gone, and the split finger was healed. There was a line on her finger. She began opening and closing her hand and making a fist. From what she said, she couldn't move her finger without pain when she arrived. Needless to say, we were all amazed at what happened. There's the beef.

> *Mark 16:17-18*

17 And these signs will accompany those who have believed: In my name they will cast out demons; they will speak with new tongues;
18 they will pick up serpents, and if they drink any deadly poison, it will not hurt them; they will lay hands on the sick, and they will recover."

In order that we would not take pride in the manifestation of God's saving power and authority working through us, God's Word tells us, *But we have this treasure in earthen vessels, so that the surpassing greatness of the power will be of God and not from ourselves; (2 Corinthians 4:7).* This "surpassing greatness of the power" is to be working in and through our lives to others for the glory of God. I believe this describes the normal Christian life. You have been authorized, not only to manifest the fruit of the Spirit, but to do the same works that Jesus did. The **authority** to display His power has been delegated to you.

The other component of this ministry is your **faith**. It may need to grow. We may have great faith or "oh ye of little faith." But your faith can certainly grow. I heard my son once say, "Faith is muscular. It grows as you exercise it." So knowing *whose* you are and *who* you are is very important for you to minister in the ministry of healing and deliverance in the kingdom.

I pray you now have greater confidence in your position in Christ and who you are as a Christian. Another important truth for all of us working in this ministry is knowing who your opposition is.

Chapter Four

Demonic Opposition

Knowing who you are in Christ is essential in the ministry of deliverance. But knowing your opposition, the devil and his demons, is equally important. Even Sun Tzu, a Chinese general and military strategist who lived around 500 B.C. is famous for advice that still applies today: "Know your enemy and know yourself and you can fight a hundred battles without disaster."

As I mentioned earlier, I played professional baseball for six years. Knowing the opposing team was very important, especially for the pitchers and catchers. One year we played against a team that had a left-hander who would hit the ball a mile if you gave him anything around the knees or belt. But it didn't take long before everyone knew that he simply could not hit a higher fastball around the letters, but he would always try. Shortly all the other teams figured that out. Guess what our pitchers threw him? High fastballs. He never gave us, or any other team, trouble after that. I think he lasted two years and was gone.

So let's take a look at who the devil and his angels are and what they can do and can't do. We must know who our opposition is and what their strengths and weaknesses are. If the demons can't hit high fastballs, that's good to know if they're standing before you, right?

Lucifer is referred to in Scripture as the fiery red dragon, the great dragon, the serpent of old, called the Devil and Satan (Rev. 12). But know this: There is only one Lucifer. He is not omnipresent (everywhere present at the same time) as the Holy Spirit is. He cannot be everywhere at the same time. He is only one spirit being. He can only be in one place at a time. Therefore, almost assuredly, we will not encounter this top spirit. He uses a host of other spirit beings. The Scriptures refer to these beings as *demons, spirits,* or *evil spirits.* These are the ones we encounter. They are also referred to as *principalities and powers, spiritual forces of wickedness, rulers and authorities.*

The word "devil" comes from the Greek word which means "to slander" or "falsely accuse." The word "Satan" means "adversary" or "enemy." The demons all fall under these descriptions. They are the ones we wrestle against. They will slander or falsely accuse you. They are the ones we come into contact with. They are our enemies and our opposition.

Where did they come from? Let me give you two possibilities. The first view is they actually were holy angels in time past, but fell from heaven when Lucifer fell (Isaiah 14:12-15). They were judged by God and are now eternally separated from God and will spend eternity in the "lake of fire" created by God for the devil and his angels (Matthew 25:41). This seems to be the most prevalent view today. The second possibility is they were created by God already evil. In other words they did not fall from heaven as holy angels, but have always been enemies of the Lord Jesus Christ. Jesus said concerning the devil, *"He was a murderer from the beginning, and does not stand in the truth because there is no truth in him" (John 8:44).* So from the beginning he was a murderer. He was never a holy angel. Fallen angel is not a biblical term. Some reject view two because that would attribute to God as the creator of evil. That's another book and a subject we will not enter into here.

What's important here is that you know clearly and certainly who the devil and his angels are presently.

What can demons do?

- **They can devour a believer.**
  1 Peter 5:8-9
  8 Be of sober spirit, be on the alert. Your adversary, the devil, prowls around like a roaring lion, seeking someone to devour.

  9 But resist him, firm in your faith...

What happens to the believer who doesn't recognize the devil's schemes? They certainly won't resist him firm in their faith and so the devouring continues.

- **They can scheme to take advantage of believers.**
  We are instructed to forgive one another. Why?
  2 Cor. 2:11
  so that no advantage would be taken of us by Satan, for we are not ignorant of his schemes.

The word "advantage" means *to have more*. Demons, by their schemes, purpose to have more. They want more access into your life, your mind and your emotions. We are not to be ignorant of this.

- **They can struggle (war) against believers.**
  Eph. 6:12
  For our struggle is not against flesh and blood, but against the rulers, against the powers, against the world forces of this darkness, against the spiritual forces of wickedness in heavenly places.

- **They can shoot flaming arrows at believers.**
  We are to hold up the shield of faith to stop these flaming arrows.

Eph. 6:16
In addition to all, taking up the shield of faith with which you will be able to extinguish all the flaming arrows of the evil one.

I believe these flaming arrows come to each of us as various demonic attacks against our person, our family or our church. They usually come as temptations, accusations and deceptions. In most cases they come to us as if *we* are thinking them. These flaming arrows may also come from the world or from the mouths of other people.

- **They can promote jealousy and selfish ambition.**
  James 3:14-15
  14 But if you have bitter jealousy and selfish ambition in your heart, do not be arrogant and so lie against the truth. 15 This wisdom is not that which comes down from above, but is earthly, natural, demonic.

- **They desire to take a place. They can gain a foothold in a believers life through a believers anger and lack of forgiveness.**
  Ephesians 4:26-27
  26 Be angry, and yet do not sin; do not let the sun go down on your anger, 27 and do not give the devil an opportunity (foothold, place).

- **The demons can blind the minds of the unbelieving.**
  2 Cor. 4:4
  in whose case the god of this world has blinded the minds of the unbelieving so that they might not see the light of the gospel of the glory of Christ, who is the image of God.

I think it's interesting that, when you stand before another person speaking to him or her about Jesus and they can't understand spiritual truth, what's really happening is the devil is somehow blinding their minds just two feet from you. Whether he's actually doing that in real time, or had set the blinders there in the past, we don't know.

Too many believers today do not understand the schemes of the devil. Too many of our friends in the church are in various stages of being devoured. Too many have not held up the shield of faith and as a result have been hit time after time by demonic flaming arrows of accusations, deceiving thoughts, negative emotions, temptations, anger, lust, hatred...etc.

Many have lived years holding on to anger and bitterness. In most cases, believers need help out of demonic strongholds. In some cases our dear Christian friends are so full of flaming arrow holes and so weak they can't hold up the shield of faith. That's where we come into this picture with love and victory. That's why I'm writing this book. I will continue to repeat this question. Will you join me and come alongside these wounded soldiers, bringing healing and freedom to our brothers and sisters in Christ?

See diagram below. It shows the progression of sin and how demonic, controlling strongholds can occur in a believers life.

The Continuum of Sin[7]

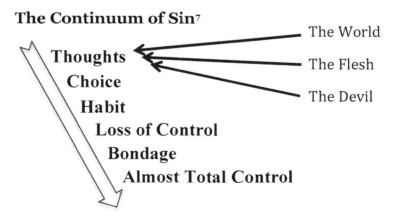

41

We all receive *thoughts* that are not our own. They come to us from the world, the flesh and the devil. These can be temptations, accusations or deceptions. To receive these thoughts is not sin. Temptation is not sin. Every person and every believer receives these thoughts. But what we do next is the issue. We have a *choice* concerning what to do with the thoughts and temptations. We can choose to allow our minds to *dwell* on them or we can *resist* them. If we make the wrong choice and entertain them, or believe them, they will keep coming our way. As we continue making wrong choices concerning these temptations, accusations or deceptions, the next thing we will find is the forming of a *habit*. This is a continuation of failure to resist the thoughts from the world, the flesh and the devil. As this continues, we then find ourselves with a *loss of control*. At this level it's very difficult to resist the devil's lies. Next we will find demonic *bondage* taking place as we continue to fail in our ability to maintain the control we desire. We find ourselves losing control over one or more sin issues in our lives. In extreme cases, demons can take *almost total control* in this area of our lives.

Sadly, a pastor I knew began this downward fall. The lusts of the flesh in the moral realm slowly gained control in and over his life. He continually yielded to the lusts of the flesh. He eventually had no ability or power to say no. He eventually lost his wife and his church. The next thing I heard was he had moved from the area, contracted a deadly sexual disease and died. Believers in every level on the "Continuum of Sin" chart need our help.

When footholds are removed the power of the temptations, accusations and deceptions is greatly diminished. The believer is much more free to make the right choice and resist the TAD coming from the world, flesh and the devil.

One last but critical point concerns what the devil *cannot* do to the believer. He can never remove you from the hands of Jesus or the Father. That's a powerful truth and a very secure, and comforting place to be.

John 10:27-30

27 My sheep hear My voice, and I know them, and they follow Me; 28 and I give eternal life to them, and they will never perish; and no one will snatch them out of My hand. 29 My Father, who has given them to Me is greater than all; and no one is able to snatch them out of the Father's hand. 30 I and the Father are one.

We just looked at who the opposition is. Let's now look at what Jesus did to the opposition.

Chapter Five

What Jesus Did To The Opposition

Wat I'm about to teach is very important for every soldier of the cross. Here are biblical truths we must know concerning what Jesus has already done to the opposition and for us.

- **Jesus rendered the devil and his angels *powerless***
  Hebrews 2:14
  Therefore, since the children share in flesh and blood, He Himself likewise also partook of the same, that through death He might render powerless him who had the power of death, that is, the devil,

- **Jesus *disarmed* the devil and his angels**
  Colossians 2:15
  When He had disarmed the rulers and authorities, He made a public display of them, having triumphed over them through Him.

- **Jesus *bound* the strong man (demonic realm)**
  Matthew 12:28-30

28 But if I cast out demons by the Spirit of God, then the kingdom of God has come upon you. 29 Or how can anyone enter the strong man's house and carry off his property, unless he first binds the strong man? And then he will plunder his house. 30 He who is not with Me is against me; and he who does not gather with Me scatters.

The **strong man** refers to the devil and his angels. His **house** refers to the world. His **property** refers to the unsaved. We are now authorized by Jesus to enter the devil's house and take from him the lost. You might say Jesus has given each Christian a license to steal.

Many of the pastors in our community are gathering together each week to pray. We're asking God for a great move of His Spirit here. We desire to see a great migration of lost men, women and children coming out of darkness into God's marvelous light. We're asking for the greatest revival on the planet, ever, to begin here. We're asking the Lord of the harvest to raise up laborers to go into the harvest fields.

Since Jesus has all authority on earth and He's commanded us to go, and since the gates of hell cannot prevail against the church, we have but one thing to do. Go! It's happening. We will continue laboring in prayer together. When the saints move out into the strongman's house, the sinners will move into the kingdom. But we've got to be realistic. It will be messy. The church is a fishing boat, not a luxury liner. These new believers will need our help. The churches will be very busy. We need to help these new believers and make them disciples. This will include removing demonic footholds.

The church in other nations often see this need. When I was in Trinidad they held a deliverance service every Thursday evening. They told me every believer needed to be set free from demonic footholds. Friends returning from Africa took a picture of a sign on a church where they ministered. It read, "Deliverance meeting" every Monday evening. This is duplicated elsewhere in the world today. Isn't this ministry also needed here in the USA?

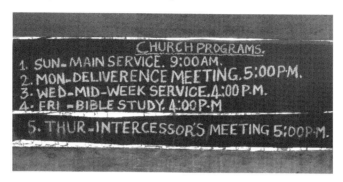

Let's continue in the truths we need to know.

- **Jesus *destroyed* the works of the devil**
  1 John 3:8
  The Son of God appeared for this purpose, to destroy the works of the devil.

This victory was won by the Son of God on the cross. The devil's works are to keep the nations - lost mankind - in darkness.

- **The gates of hell will *not prevail* against the church**
  Matthew 16:18-19
  Jesus said, I *will build My church; and the gates of Hell will not prevail against it.*

- **We overwhelmingly conquer through Christ**
  Romans 8:37
  But in all these things we overwhelmingly conquer through Him who loved us.

Let's review what Christ has done to the devil and his demons for us:

- Jesus rendered them powerless... but empowered us.
- Jesus disarmed them... but armed us.
- Jesus bound them (tied up)... but set us free.
- Jesus destroyed their works... but empowers our work.
  Hell's gates cannot stop us. We are more than conquerors.

Therefore, since Jesus has all authority on earth (Matt. 28:18), He told *us* to go, and as we are going we are to make disciples of all nations. Why can we do this? Because the devil has been bound. His gates cannot hold us out. We have been given authority to do all this and *"to tread on serpents and scorpions, and over all the power of the enemy, and nothing will injure you. 20 Nevertheless do not rejoice in this, that the spirits are subject to you, but rejoice that your names are recorded in heaven"* *(Luke 10:19-20).* We follow behind our commander...bringing with us the spoils of war – men, women, and children rescued from the domain of darkness and transferred to the kingdom of God's dear Son. The enemy has been disarmed. Their works destroyed. What are we waiting for?

We do not fight <u>for</u> victory...we fight <u>from</u> victory! The battle is already won!

So here's a "new normal" for the church in our day. New believers coming from the devil's house will need teaching, baptism, deliverance, blessing, healing, the filling of the Spirit, all wrapped in much love and patience. We must lead them to the presence of God, from which comes a desire for His Word, prayer, worship and a passion to tell others about their Jesus and His saving, cleansing power.

This is <u>not</u> God verses Satan.
Some believe there are two equal forces battling it out, while mankind is held in the balance. In this scenario, God takes risks with us, not being able to accomplish His desired end.

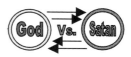

But here is the biblical truth:
God is ruler over all, and all the affairs of this world, including the devil and his angels. He accomplishes His desired end.

God is in complete control over this world, and what happens during our lives here.

> *Lamentations 3:38*
> *Is it not from the mouth of the Most High that both calamities and good things come? NIV*

> *Isaiah 45:7*
> *I form the light and create darkness, I bring prosperity and create disaster; I, the LORD, do all these things. NIV*

> *Ephesians 1:11*
> *(God) works out everything in conformity with the purpose of His will*

As we lock onto this Biblical truth, we can understand and live in the following reality. *What then shall we say to these things? If God is for us, who is against us? (Rom. 8:30)*

Chapter Six

Deliverance Meeting Outline

We are now ready to begin outlining a typical meeting with a fellow believer who wants to see if what they are experiencing may be due to a demonic foothold in their life. Let me say this first: I really don't know if that's the case until I actually meet and begin the various steps and actually confront a spirit.

One day a young Christian girl, I'll call her Janice, called me. She was struggling with depression and nagging thoughts. She asked me, "Could it be this is not just me, but empowered by an enemy of the Lord Jesus Christ?" I answer this kind of question with, "It could be. There's only one way to really find out. Can we schedule a meeting and explore the possibility?"

I always have at least one other lady with me when I meet with ladies and one other man when I meet with men, although I sometimes meet with men alone. The third person prays, listens and takes notes. The purpose of the notes are two-fold: 1) To have a written account of our meetings and 2) to record possible confrontation areas to be explore during the final phase of our meeting.

The agenda is simple, although it often takes 2-3 hours to complete the steps. I follow the biblical format of James 4:7. *"Submit therefore to God. Resist the devil and he will flee from you."* Let me outline a typical first meeting. Then I'll go into greater detail in the next chapter.

1. Initial Conversation. Smile, shake hands. Make them feel as comfortable as possible. Often they will be friends in the church, but they will still feel uncomfortable.

2. Why are you here? After all have been seated in a comfortable chair have them tell their story. What has been happening in their life? Why are they meeting with you? Begin taking notes at this point.

3. My position explained. At this point I explain that I will assume the issues they are experiencing are coming from an enemy foothold. It may not be so, but from this point I will assume it is. It gives me freedom to minister.

4. Keep the "radio" on. They must agree to tell me what's on their "radio" – that is any contrary thoughts, negative emotions, or physical hurts or pains that appear as we talk.

5. Talk to God: Pray and invite the Holy Spirit to work and bring healing to this Christian man, woman or child.

6. Find possible doors: Explain that demons cannot gain a foothold and affect our lives at their will. They must have a door. We try to find doors in their past that may have opened demonic access to their life. If we find a door, we can remove any devouring enemy and close the door.

7. Submit to Christ. In this step I use Neil T. Anderson's *the Steps to FREEDOM IN CHRIST[5]*. This is a great resource to help the believer renounce and confess past actions and unconfessed sins they have committed. This is usually the most time-consuming stage of the process.

8. Authority and confrontation. I have learned that, in most cases, demons must be confronted. Demonic footholds are removed during this confrontation.

9. Follow up.
This deliverance ministry is normally a process and not an event.

Some have described it as removing one layer of onion at a time. You continue to schedule meetings until all the layers have been removed. I will always schedule a second meeting to get a report of how the person is doing. The person tells me where there were victories, temptations and failures. This guides me where to continue the confrontation stage. The follow up meetings are mostly confrontation stage issues.

I will now elaborate a little more on each of these nine points. Join me in a typical first meeting.

Chapter Seven

Normal Deliverance Meeting

1. Initial Conversation

Normally, people are unfamiliar with this process and therefore apprehensive and somewhat fearful as the first meeting begins. People have seen too many movies and heard too much misinformation out there. I want them to feel as comfortable and relaxed as possible. I smile, shake hands, and warmly greet my friend. I use my home on occasion; but most often I use one of two quite rooms in our church where there are no phones or casual traffic. We sit in cushioned rocking chairs so that all are as comfortable as possible. I assure them they are free to take a timeout any time they desire...for water, the restroom or just a break. Several believers I've met with have needed to take breaks for their smoking addiction. That's ok. Don't judge them. I recommend that you, as the leader, take a break at least every hour. This process is taxing for your friend and you'll need a breather, too. Normally the first meeting will last three to four hours, but occasionally more or less. Some individuals are not physically or emotionally strong enough to go long periods of time. That's alright – adjust your schedule to accommodate their needs.

I will sit directly across from the person, about 4-6 feet away. I position myself so there are no windows or motions behind me to distract attention. My assistant sits off to my right between my friend and me, and out of my friend's direct line of sight. I do not recommend taking more than one person through the deliverance ministry at the same time.

Explain that all three of you are meeting as a team. We need to work together having one purpose, to do what the Bible says. *Submit therefore to God, resist the devil and he will flee from you (James 4:7).* People with demonic footholds in their lives need encouragement and help to do this. The end goal is to free them from all footholds and teach them how to be alert, to watch, to submit to God, to take every thought captive and resist the devil throughout their lives.

At this point have them read and sign the "Ministry Release Form" found at the back of this book. The information on this form is important for them to know. So be sensitive, friendly and encouraging toward this friend who has come to you for ministry.

2. Why Are You Here? Their Story

I then ask them what prompted their request to meet with me. They will express what's going on in their life and what they have been experiencing. My associate begins to take notes at this point. I'm looking for helpful things I need to remember and possible points where the enemy may have gained a foothold. I keep a record of our meetings to record any possible doors or confrontation areas. Please remember, these meetings are always confidential. In this book when I share a story, I have permission to do so or I have changed the names.

Becky told me she was having distracting thoughts during times of Bible reading and prayer. She also often had migraine headaches and shared with me that she fought jealousy toward her husband. She wanted to know if this could be empowered by the enemy. I told her, "It's possible. There's one way to find out." From just this initial conversation I now have three confrontation points to be aware of: Distracting thoughts, migraines and jealousy. My partner will write these down on the note paper.

Some people have come to see me with the wrong motives. One husband told me that his wife made him come and see me after she caught him looking at pornography on the computer. That's the wrong motivation. The person must "want" to meet with you. Their motives are very important. I've had several people over the years who came with wrong motives. One person came to me because they loved the attention they received in the meeting! Wrong motive meetings are mostly non-productive.

3. Your Stance Explained

At this point, I explain that I will take the stance that this is a demonic foothold issue. I'm going to *assume* that from this point forward we're dealing with a demonic foothold. I then explain if we find it's not a foothold there's no harm, no foul. This gives me the freedom to push forward. Let me say here that in most cases it has been a demonic foothold. I have a strong desire to help my friends and fellow Christian believers. So I humbly take that stance. You, too, want to find and remove any and all footholds that the enemy may have gained in your Christian friend's life.

4. Keep the Radio On

What I'm about to say here is crucial. Demons are not dummies. They know you are meeting to remove their foothold, their place. Therefore, the spirits will most likely scheme together and attempt to stop that from happening. These acts of resistance will happen in the following three arenas. Therefore, the person needs to tell you what's happening in these three different locations: I refer to them as **the radio**.

- Their mind (thoughts)
- Their emotions
- Their body

Mind:

At this point I explain to my Christian friend that their mind is like a **radio**. It's a receiver. It receives thoughts placed there by the world, flesh and the devil (demons). In some cases, our friends have listened to these thoughts their entire lives. They often cannot distinguish these thoughts from their own thoughts.

I ask the person to tell me any contrary
thoughts that comes to their mind.

I tell them those thoughts are not their thoughts. I want to know what they hear (think). Why? That together we might do what the Bible says, to judge the thoughts and by doing so, stop the power of those lies. There's power in those thoughts while it stays within their mind. They've been listening and believing them a long time. Sharing the thought and applying biblical truth to it removes it's power. The Bible tells us to judge our thoughts. Often the person can't judge those thoughts themselves. They believe it's their own thoughts. You must help them judge the thoughts. Ask them to **keep the radio on**. In other words, if a negative thought pops into their mind, I ask them to share with me what they just thought...anytime and every time. I will then help them judge that thought.

One person told me, "I'm thinking I've got to get out of here." I said, "Thanks for sharing that thought. That's sounds like an enemy thought, doesn't it? You're here because you want to be, right?" "That's right." "Let's keep going and keep the radio on." Make sure your partner makes a note of that thought. You will want to address the source of that thought during the confrontation stage.

During a recent meeting, my Christian friend John said, "Dave, I just received a thought." I replied, "What was it." "I just thought, 'This isn't going to work.'" I thanked him for telling me and also told him the thought was most likely a lie from the enemy. I asked my associate to record that thought. I will go back to it during the Confrontation Stage. For an example, let's jump to the Confrontation Stage now.

During the Confrontation Stage I stated, "I want the spirit that said earlier, 'This isn't going to work' to get up here and look at me. I command your presence before me." At this point I assume the spirit is before me. In most cases the spirit is there. Sometimes the person can sense the spirit is there. I asked the spirit the questions that demonstrate my authority over him. "I command the truth to this question. Do you understand that you have been defeated by Jesus Christ on the cross?" The spirit answered into the mind of my friend, "Yes." John told me what he heard. Next I replied, "Do you understand that John belongs to Jesus Christ and not to you?" The spirit answered, "No." I said, "That's a lie. We both know that he does. Now answer that question again...truthfully. Do you understand that John belongs to Jesus Christ and not to you?" Then came a reluctant "Yes." "Do you have any grounds to remain in John's life?" "No." "Then leave. Release John's mind, his emotions and this foothold you've had and get out of here. Go right through that wall (I point to the exterior wall). You're not staying. Leave our presence. Now. Go! Go where Jesus sends you...now!" In most cases demons respond and obey this kind of verbiage.

It's very important to keep asking the person, "Is there anything on the radio?" or "How are you feeling?" Their contrary feelings and thoughts have been part of their lives for years and in some cases for their whole life. They may need constant reminders to share with you what's going on. In many cases they have never been able to distinguish between demonic thoughts and their own thoughts.

One man stopped our meeting and told me his head was hurting. I replied to the spirit, "Leave his head alone. Stop the headache...now." He smiled in amazement and told me, "It stopped. It's not hurting anymore." God's power is greater than demonic power. Your job is to stop what the demons are trying to do, which is to hinder or stop the meeting. Use your authority. You don't have to yell at them. But firmly state what they are going to do or not do. Statements like, "You have to stop" or, "You must stop" are not as firm as they could be. A stronger statement to a demon is simply, "Stop!" or, "I command you to stop what you're doing. Now!" Christ is in you and greater is He who is in you than he who is in the world. Remember, Jesus said, everyone who believes in Me will do the same works that I have done (John 14:12). That includes having authority over demons.

As I noted earlier, I normally do not confront demons before the confrontation stage. There are times, however, when I have to. I once had an initial meeting with a teenager named Jane, and her mother. The young girl was a believer who loved Jesus Christ, but was having difficulty with fear and distracting thoughts. As we were talking she was being interrupted by various thoughts. As we continued to talk, she kept getting interference. I could see she was troubled. That spirit was greatly hindering our meeting. She told me what was happening in her mind and emotions.

I said, "That sounds like the enemy." I asked her if I could confront that spirit. She said, "Please do." I told her to tell me what she hears in her mind in reply to my questioning. I said, "I want to know who you are that keeps interfering with our meeting. I command you, enemy of the Lord Jesus Christ, to come forward right now. Get up here. Look into my eyes. You'll only speak into Jane's mind. I want to know who you are. What's your assigned purpose in Jane's life?" She heard the word "fear." I said,

"Are you a spirit called Fear?" "Yes" was the reply. I said, "I command you to tell me the truth. Do you have any grounds to remain in Jane's life?" "No" came the answer. I then said (commanded), "Then you leave quietly...now. You're not staying here. Go where Jesus sends you. Leave! Go right through that wall (pointing toward the wall). You'll never come back. Get out now! Leave this child of God...Now."

Jane smiled. She told me she felt that spirit leave. I don't trust the spirits, so I checked and asked if that spirit of Fear was still here. "If you're still here, we're still talking. You're not hiding on me, or tricking me. If you're here answer me now. Are you still here?" No answer! I said to Jane, "That's all there is to it." She had a big smile on her face and we continued to talk, unhindered. We worked through the rest of the ministry process. I met with Jane a couple of days later. She became free from a few other bothersome spirits. She continues to do well to this day. So the radio is contrary thoughts you hear in your mind. Next, it's also what you feel emotionally on the negative side.

Emotions:

I once met with a friend in my church who was struggling with an eating disorder called bulimia. Both she and her husband were somewhat skeptical about this whole thing. During our meeting, she received the emotion of hatred toward me. She struggled with that emotion. After several minutes of battling this emotion she finally reported what was happening on the radio. She had actually been able to work through the following thought process. Even though she was feeling hatred toward me, she reasoned in her mind that she didn't hate me because we were friends. She knew at that point that this was not her but an enemy doing that to her. She then shared these thoughts with me. At that point she realized that this really was a spiritual warfare issue. Both she and her husband were completely on board from that point forward. It's important the person is "on board" with you.

When people come to me they are already on board. In the case above I went to my friend to try to help her. "On board" means skepticism is removed. This sometimes happens when the enemy tries to stop or hinder the meeting and you use God-given authority to stop them.

One older man shared with me he was feeling the emotion of fear. I said, "If this is a spirit of fear or one who's causing fear, leave this man alone. Stop doing that to him." The fear instantly left. A tiny smile came to his face. We continued.

It's important that you know what's on the radio so you can stop what the enemy is attempting to do. So the radio consists of **mind** (what contrary thoughts is your friend thinking), **emotions** (what negative feelings are they having emotionally? And the third component is what's happening to your **physical body**.

Body:

Often an individual will tell me during our meeting that they're experiencing a headache. I simply command the spirit causing that pain to stop and leave this person alone. In most cases, the spirits do stop. Often, I see a smile on the person's face when the pain stops so quickly. They are then on board even more than before. It's often exciting for the Christian friend you are taking through the deliverance process to see a manifestation of God's authority and power in their own lives. This can happen anytime during the meeting when a physical pain comes upon the person you're meeting with. Take authority over the spirit that's causing the pain and tell him to leave this person alone. Allow me to restate...use a direct, strong command rather than, "You must stop that pain" or "You have to stop this pain." Be as direct as you can. "Stop that headache. Now."

One of your jobs is to stop the demons from derailing the deliverance process. You can do that because the Holy Spirit is in you. Do not be afraid to use your authority. Make sure you record that pain for the confrontation stage.

Let me fast-forward to the confrontation stage. At one point I would ask, *"I want the spirit that caused that headache earlier to get before me right now. Look at me and answer my questions. I command the truth from you. Do you understand that you were defeated when Jesus disarmed the rulers and authorities and made a public display of them, having triumphed over them?"* "Yes." *"Do you understand that (person's name) belongs to this same Jesus Christ and not to you?"* "Yes." *"Do you have any spiritual grounds to remain in (person's name) life?"* "No." *"What have you been assigned to accomplish in (person's name) life?"*

I'll receive answers like, "To defeat them." "To stop their growth." "To destroy their marriage." "Bring pain or fear to their lives." "Kill them, destroy them." Often the name of the spirit is associated with what they've been assigned to accomplish in this person's life. If the spirit has been assigned to destroy the person, the spirit's name could be Destroy, Destruction, or Death. With demons, their names correspond to their character or what they are attempting to accomplish, just as Bible names correspond to an individual's character and actions. At this point, I take them through the verbiage to leave this person's life, as I explained earlier.

Caution is in order here: All demons are experts at lying and deceiving. That's their nature. I'm always cautious with information I receive from demons. But the Lord is in charge here. So I proceed with the information I receive from them, but always with caution.

One day I was training two of my church friends how to bring freedom to their fellow believers. As a demonstration, I was taking one of them through the Steps To Freedom deliverance ministry process. After two hours we completed the steps and came to the final confrontation stage. In one of the Steps, I noticed he had identified several items he was fearful of.

I explained what I was then going to do in the confrontation stage. He said, "Let's go for it." First I confronted the spirit of fear. I commanded, "I want to know if there is a spirit of fear here. Get up here and look at me." Instantly he bent over in pain. He said his stomach felt like one big cramp. I told that spirit to stop, to leave him alone. Then, I went through the process of commanding the spirit to answer my questions and then to release him and leave him. It wasn't long before this spirit was gone. We ran into two other spirits of fear. Each one caused that stomach cramp pain. They all left. My friend's eyes were opened to the reality of this ministry and he was on board in a much deeper way. He has now been helping me as my partner. I love to have his assistance.

The job of the one you're counseling is to let you know if pain is occurring. Your job is to determine if the pain's source is demonic, then to confront it and remove it.

Ok, let's review. From this point forward, I ask the person I'm meeting with to keep their radio on, and to tell me what they're receiving. Their mind is like a radio, in that it receives outside signals. They must report what they receive in three areas:

a. Every negative **thought** that enters their mind. Demons will speak into our minds. They often give us thoughts in the first-person-singular, such as, "I'm ugly", "I'm no good", or "I can't do this." If we believe those lies, they have much power over us. If the person tells me their thoughts, I can help judge them and depower them. I refer to this as the **radio**. They must keep the radio on and report every negative thought. I let them know those kinds of thoughts are not their thoughts. That, in itself, can bring peace to our friends.

b. The radio also includes whatever negative **emotions** are taking place within them, such as fear, anxiety, hatred, panic etc. If this happens, as it sometimes does, I simply tell the spirit or spirits causing this to stop and leave the person alone. Then, as I proceed, I often remind them to keep that radio on. Remember to take notes of any interference so you can go back and confront and remove that spirit during the confrontation stage.

c. The radio also includes how they are feeling **physically**. I want to know if they are experiencing a headache, tightness in the chest, or neck pain, etc. I then command the spirit causing that to stop. Continue reminding your friend to keep the radio on. And again, remember to take notes concerning any enemy interruption. You will want to go back and challenge the spirit that caused that interruption during the confrontation stage. If the interruption is prevailing, confront that spirit immediately. Confront it with questions and commands such as below. You are in control, not that spirit.

- "Do you understand that you've been defeated by the Lord Jesus Christ on the cross?"
- "Do you understand that (John) belongs to the Lord Jesus Christ and not to you?"
- "Do you have any grounds to remain in (John's) life?"
- "What have you been assigned to accomplish in this person's life?"
- "Are you here because of any curse?" If so, break the curse. I say, "I break this curse in Jesus' name, and right now I break every bond associated with this curse."
- "I command you, in Jesus' name, to release (John). Release his mind. Release his emotions and release your foothold and get out of here. Go right through that wall, now. Go where Jesus sends you, and you'll never come back. Go...now..." Our job is to remove the spirit.

- I don't trust them. They may pretend to go. "Is that spirit I was addressing still here in (John's) life? If you're still here, we're still talking. Answer me!"
- Continue with such questions and commands until you're assured that spirit is no longer present.

5. Talk To God

Before I begin the Steps To Peace, I always pray and invite the Lord to work and His Spirit to give wisdom and power for the healing of the person who has come to me. There are several things I always include in my opening prayer.

1) I ask God to seal the room so that no spiritual enemies of the Lord Jesus Christ can enter to disrupt our meeting. I normally ask Him to send His angels to accomplish that.

2) Dedicate your time to God. Ask Him to accomplish all that He desires. Ask Him to bring healing to your friend who has come to you for help. Ask God that you all may hear His promptings and the conviction and voice of the Holy Spirit during your meeting together. It's good to be listening for direction during your meetings. When the unseen enemy is working, so is the unseen Holy Spirit. Listen for Him throughout your meeting.

3) I also command that if there are any **shared spirits** here they will not leave the room unless I command them to go. What are shared spirits? These are spirits who have a place, a foothold in more than one person. Several times I have been confronting a spirit, when all of a sudden, the spirit is gone, only to find them back the next week. I learned they were shared spirits that just took off to their other victim(s) when they were about to be commanded to go. My command to stay has worked. I haven't lost any since I've been commanding them to stay until I tell them to go. I'll often ask a spirit I'm confronting if it is a shared spirit. When I command them to go, I also command them to not return to their shared person.

Understanding the sovereignty of God is very important in this ministry. The reason your Christian brother or sister is sitting before you is because God has brought them there. This is God's work. I believe if God has them sitting there with me, He's going to bring healing to them, eventually. This is always my mindset. This is what I know to be true about God. The healing may be a process. It may take several meetings, but God is in control and He has our brother or sister there for healing, teaching and exhortation. He will use you to accomplish all of this. So I know that when someone sits down with me, God is already working. He's asking me to join with Him. What a privilege this is! I know that the enemy's time is over for the child of God before me.

This is God's work. During this healing process please understand that God is not only teaching your friend, but you as well. The teaching is as important as the healing. When both are combined, it's a wonderful result.

Remember who you are in Christ as you dedicate your time together in prayer.

1. You are a child of God. Have child-like faith.
2. You've been given authority to *trample on serpents and scorpions, and over all the power of the enemy, and nothing shall by any means hurt you (Luke 10:19).*

Don't be rejoicing in the fact that demons are subject to you. It's true that they are...

Nevertheless do not rejoice in this, that the spirits are subject to you, but rather rejoice because your names are written in heaven."
In that hour Jesus rejoiced in the Spirit and said, "I thank You, Father, Lord of heaven and earth, that You have hidden these things from the wise and prudent

and revealed them to babes. NKJV (Luke 10:20-21)

Be one of those babes in Christ. Aren't you glad you are not one of the "wise and prudent" Jesus is referring to? You are a babe, a child of God. Have child-like faith as you proceed to bring healing to your friends. May we bring even greater freedom and power and passion to the saints.

6. Find Possible Doors

At this point, I explain that demons cannot gain a foothold in our lives at their will. They must have a door. It's here that I try to find the kind of doors which may have opened demonic access, or footholds, into their life.

I go through a checklist of their family and personal history. Remember to have your partner keep notes about anything that is revealed.

Family History

- **What do they know about their parents and grandparents?**
  Sin and demonic issues of parents or grandparents can be transferred into children or grandchildren at birth. Ancestral sin and bloodline curses are very common, but they can easily be broken.
- **Was there abuse (physical, sexual, emotional) in their ancestry?**
  Any kind of abuse can open doors. Many of God's people who come to me have abuse in their family's background. If the perpetrator has demonic foothold issues in his/her life, this abuse can open doors into the victim's life.
- **Were they adopted or in foster care?**
  Ask if they have any information about their birth parents or grandparents. This is important information for a later

confrontation stage.

Personal History

- **Eating habits** (bulimia, anorexia, compulsive eating)
- **Addictions** (cigarettes, drugs, alcohol)
- **Prescription medications** (what for?)
- **Sleeping patterns, dream and nightmares**
- **Sexual, physical or emotional abuse**
- **Thought life** (obsessive, blasphemous, condemning and distracting thoughts; poor concentration; fantasy; suicidal thoughts; fearful; jealous; confused; guilt and shame)
- **Mental interference** during church, prayer or Bible study
- **Emotional life** (anger, anxiety, depression, bitterness and fear)
- **Spiritual journey** (salvation: when, how and assurance)

These are found in Neil T. Anderson's ***the steps to FREEDOM IN CHRIST***, P. 5.

Eating disorders may indicate a door was opened in the past. Those with eating disorders are being deceived when looking at themselves in the mirror. They are seeing and hearing in their minds something not true.

Addictions also indicate a possible door. Any addictive, compulsive behavior in a believer's life is likely to be empowered by the demonic realm.

Nightmares and irregular sleeping patterns may also indicate a foothold occurred in an individual's past.

Abuse must also be looked at as a possible door opening for the enemies of Jesus Christ. The abuser is certainly struggling with demonic footholds in his or her life. The demons can access into a victims life during the abuse. My wife and I met with a friend of ours who had been sexually abused by a motorcycle gang member. This happened during the Christmas season. For many years she could not enjoy the Christmas season with her family. We removed the spirits that took access in her life through that abuse. She never had an issue after that and greatly enjoyed her Savior and family during Christmas.

Mental interference or distracting thoughts may also indicate enemy activity. Take good notes here.

Returning to Earl's story (p. 29-30), it was during this preliminary personal history that he explained his past anger and how it manifested in his life, his work and his marriage. We went through *the Steps To Freedom in Christ* which strengthened Earl and taught him to submit himself to God. I believe it also weakened the spirits that we encountered during the confrontation stage.

7. Submit To Christ (Steps To Freedom)

Now we begin *the Steps To Freedom* which greatly assists our friends to submit themselves to Christ. This process also is a form of resisting the devil. This section will be difficult without having a copy of the *Steps To Freedom*. Go to footnotes #6 and order a copy.

- I explain to each person that they will be reading aloud the prayers in bold print.
- I also ask them if they believe reading scripted prayers is effective. Most agree that reading prayers is as effective as spontaneous prayers if they are read with a spirit of agreement and sincerity.
- I remind them to read with a prayerful attitude.
- Checklists follow most of the steps in Anderson's booklet. I ask them to complete each checklist silently. I also request that if they are going to err on these check-lists, err on checking the box rather than leaving it blank. Remember

also, we're looking for demonic foothold doors from the past. If the checklist item applied in their past, they should check it.

Begin by asking your Christian friend to read aloud the prayer for **Step 1**. Then have them complete the check-list. They may not know what some of the checklist words are. I simply explain to them, "If you don't know what it means, you were probably not involved with it."

After they have completed the checklist, take them to the next page. There's a prayer of confession and a renouncement of the things they checked on the previous page. Have them pray the prayer aloud and have them include all the things they checked. It's that simple. In most cases people will fly through this first step. I always tell them, "Great job. You did well." And then I ask, "Anything on the radio?"

There are also 5 questions on that page. Have your friend read each question silently and tell you if there are any "yes" answers. Some of these you will have already discussed. Be sure your associate takes notes for any "yes" answers.

The Kingdom of Darkness and Kingdom of Light section I do not use unless the person has been involved in the occult.

Move on to **Step 2**...Deception. We've all been deceived by the father of lies. This may have opened a door in the past. As in Step 1, ask them to pray the prayer aloud. After the prayer I ask again, "Anything on the radio?" Now have them work through the first checklist. Then ask them to pray the prayer at the bottom of the checklist and include the things they checked in their prayer.

Remember, you are looking for possible doors from their *past,* so if any of the checklist items applied at some point in their past, have them check the box. It may not apply to them presently, but may have been what they believed in their past. Have them check it and confess it. Work through all three check lists, including the prayers following each list.

Again, encourage them, "Good job. Anything on the radio when you were going through the confession prayers?" One man told me he had a hard time reading because the words became blurry. I asked if that normally happens when he reads anything at other times. He answered, "No." Because of my assumption that this issue was demonic, I had my partner make a note of this. I will address the spirit that caused this later. I also want to make sure the blurred vision doesn't continue to happen. It didn't happen again in this case, but if it had I would have stopped right then and told that spirit, "You enemy of the Lord Jesus Christ, if you're causing the blurriness, stop. You're not going to do that again to (person's name)." Then continue.

Next are the **Statements of Truth**. I have the friend before me read each one of these statements aloud. It's what we believe. It's biblical truth. It's actually a great Bible study if you took the time to look up each verse. But that's not why you are meeting. I'll stop after the forth statement and ask a couple of questions. "Are you reading with comprehension?" Have you ever found yourself reading something while your mind was thinking about something else? We can all do that. So I make sure that's not happening here. Next I ask, "Is there anything on the radio?" Oftentimes, this is where the devil will interrupt. Demons hate biblical truth.

One day my wife and I met with a married couple. The wife was working through these steps with me. When she began reading the *Statements of Truth* she passed out! Yes, you heard me correctly. Somehow the devil did that and it completely ended our meeting. I couldn't stop the spirit from doing that to her. Admittedly, I was somewhat a beginner at this point. We tried again a few day later and the same thing happened. These were stronger spirits than I realized. My wife and I spent the next two weeks in fasting and prayer. I fasted from food for 4 days and a few days later for 2 days. This lady was struggling with an eating disorder. When she looked in the mirror she was seeing deceptive lies from the enemy. She saw herself as overweight in the mirror, when just the opposite was true. Her life centered around these thoughts. The scales in the bathroom were in frequent use. The demons had control of her thoughts. She was continually dwelling on her weight and looks.

One of the spirits we encountered was called "Control." Even without the woman present, my wife and I came against that spirit and many others during our private prayer times. We prayed, asking God to bring healing into her mind, emotions and body. We also used our authority to come against the demons. I would say, *"You spirits deceiving this woman, especially the spirit called 'Control,' you have been disarmed and defeated by the Lord Jesus Christ. Jesus came to destroy the works of the enemy. That's you. We bind you to silence and weakness in this person's life...in her mind and emotions. We claim healing for her. We believe this is God's will and that we have the petitions we desire (1 John 5:14-15). Be quite in her mind."*

After two weeks, there was a knock on our door. It was her. She had her bathroom scales in her hands and she handed it to us. What a victory! We met again shortly after that, and this time the demons could not take her out. She's healthy and doing very well many years later.

Continue through the Statements of Truth to **Step 3.** Anger and unforgiveness are devastating issues in the church today. They represent a huge doorway for demons.

After praying the prayer, stop and talk about anger and forgiveness. How can you be angry and not sin?

Ephesians 4:26

26 Be angry, and yet do not sin; do not let the sun go down on your anger,

In other words, we sin by letting the sun go down while still angry. Deal with it before bedtime. Why?

27 and do not give the devil an opportunity

The word opportunity means "place" or "foothold". Not dealing with anger, not forgiving, living with bitterness and hurt can open up a place for the devil in our lives. We "deal" with it by forgiving each other. Three of the most powerful words in the English language are, "I forgive you."

This is a good place to talk about forgiveness. Encourage the person you are meeting with that forgiving is an act of obedience. We choose to forgive or not. It's not based on our emotion. We forgive by faith. We were not created to keep others on our hook. The person who hurt you is on God's hook. That's where they belong, not on yours. Let them off your hook.

Forgiveness is not forgetting. But it does result in healing. We don't heal to then forgive. We forgive to heal. We live by faith. Our responses are based upon faith, in obedience to God.

I ask them, "Is there anyone you could put on that list of people you need to forgive?" This would include those they are angry with, hurt by or have resentment toward. This could go back to their childhood. Have them write their names on a piece of paper that you provide. Give them time at this point. When they have finished, I give them two more possibilities for them to consider. First, are they angry at themselves? Some people can't forgive themselves because of the things they have done. They need to let themselves off the hook also. Second, are they angry at God? Some people are angry at God for difficult things He has allowed in their lives.

I will then say, "Let me ask God to reveal to you if there are any others that He wants you to include on your list." Then I pray, "God, will you reveal to (person's name) if there is any other person that needs to be put on their list to be forgiven?" It's amazing how often they, at that moment, think of another person to include.

I continue this step by saying something like this. "It's been my experience that the Lord may reveal others for you to forgive in the days to come." It's also important that they know they must keep current in this area of forgiveness. Forgive often.

One person said to me, "Dave, I'm going back home and will face my husband. I know I have forgiven him here, but it won't last very long before he chops me down again. I mean how often do I forgive him?" I answered, "How often did Jesus say we were to forgive one another? Seven times?" She answered, "70 times 7." "That's right. That means every time, all the time."

I now construct the prayer for them. It's simple. It goes something like this.

"Lord Jesus, I forgive (name the person) for (what they did or failed to do)."

Be specific. Go through the whole list one at a time. Remember, it's not, "Lord, help me to forgive..." I'll stop them if I hear that. It's "Lord, I forgive..."

One more item needs to be addressed here. Letting the sun go down on your anger and not forgiving is described by a three-letter word in Scripture. It's called SIN. It also needs to be addressed. I also have them confess their sin of anger, failing to forgive or bitterness.

Forgiveness is a big issue in the church today. Every time I preach on forgiveness it touches a nerve in many people. As I explained earlier, I've seen much healing come to individuals through just completing this forgiveness step.

You are now well on your way to helping your believing friend who is struggling with one or more areas in their life. They are submitting themselves to God and resisting the devil.

Continue and complete **Step 4** and **Step 5.** Pride is one of the foundations of sin in our lives. The prayer in Step 5 is my favorite. I enjoy praying silently along with the person who is reading the prayer. Have your friend complete the checklists in these steps and include the checked items in the prayers at the bottom of those steps.

Remember to ask if there is anything on the radio. This would include contrary thoughts, emotions and any physical issues or pains, such as headaches, stomach pain, chest pain, etc.

It's important that they share any negative thoughts with you. If those negative thoughts stay in their mind they may hurt the healing process. When they speak them out and put them there on that imaginary table you can help them judge that thought. Coming against the lie with scriptural truth removes the power of the lie. They need help to out-truth the devil's lies.

You are now ready to continue to **Step 6.** This section deals with moral sin issues. There are two sides to this step. After praying the first prayer, have them complete the first checklist. Often all the items in the first check list will be checked. I tell them that I would have to check them all. They're not the Lone Ranger here. Have your friend confess those sins in the prayer that follows the list.

Now move to page 17. This is the sexual sin door. Sexual sin is a very active door for the enemy for both men and women. Note: When I meet with ladies I will have them read the first prayer on this page. I will then read the next paragraph. I will then turn the rest of conversation to my lady partner and I will leave the room. I think it's easier for ladies to talk to ladies about sexual matters. Then they will confess and renounce all these sins in the next prayer on page 17. It's important for this person to renounce every immoral use of their body, whether it was done to them (rape, incest, sexual molestation) or willingly by them (pornography, masturbation, sexual immorality).

After this process I'm invited back into the room. If there is a prominent door possibility my partner will let me know. It may be that I will need to confront a spirit in this moral realm during the confrontation stage.

Remember, these steps are helping them to submit themselves to God. That, in itself, is a form of resisting the devil. After they renounce every sin, by using the second prayer, then complete this step by praying through the next prayer, the third prayer on this page. Following are other good prayers dealing with specific issues. Use them if they apply.

You are now ready to continue on to address fear. **Fear** issues are very common with many of God's people. I always introduce each step with a sentence or two. Fear is a possible door for the enemy.

I once had a series of meetings to help a young girl I will call Jill. Jill had become involved in a Satanic Coven. The lady who reached her with the gospel was my partner. Jill had many demonic strongholds in her life. She could not even get through the Steps to Freedom. There was too much demonic activity. The first couple of hours I was only addressing demons.

As I was addressing one of the spirits, it became very vocal and loud through Jill. I calmly responded to the spirit and told it to stop and be silent. But at that moment I noticed my partner was grabbing her head bending over in her chair in pain and agony. The demon was somehow able to do that to her. How could that happen? It's never happened before. I commanded that spirit to stop and to depart from my friend and leave her alone. It obeyed. The spirit came from Jill, to my partner, and then back to Jill. But the pain and grimacing was now over.

I wanted to know how that could happen to my partner. We learned that my partner became fearful during that spirit's loud vocal escapade. It was the fear that opened the door. I had my partner renounce and confess her fear. It never happened again. What was the final outcome? Jill gained more and more freedom. At one point Jill asked me, "Dave, how do I know who I am?" She'd been controlled so much by demons she didn't know who she really was. I said, "Jesus will show you and teach you who you really are, Jill." We met several times and God used us to bring freedom to Jill.

In one of our last meetings with Jill, she began to tell me what she was seeing in her minds eye. "Dave, I see a man on a white horse in the distance. He's also dressed in white and has a sword on his side. Dave, could that be Jesus?" I said, "I don't know. It could be." She continued telling us what she was seeing.

"He's riding up to me. He's getting off his horse." I was not expecting what happened next. All of a sudden Jill gave out a loud scream. Then she stopped and slumped over. I just sat there waiting. Finally I said, "Jill, what happened?" She raised up and continued. "He got off His horse. He walked over to me with His sword in His hand. He raised His sword over His head with both hands holding it and brought it down. That's when I screamed. He divided me into two people. Angels came and took the other half of me away. I also saw demons running everywhere trying to get away. Angels grabbed them up and put them into a box. The box had two poles that went through rings on opposite sides of the box. When they gathered the last demon into the box, two angels carried the box away. The earth split apart and I saw fire coming up out of the opening. They dropped the box into the opening where the fire burned. Then the earth came back together again and the angles disappeared." All we could do is look at each other and smile.

It was wonderful to see what God did for Jill. Remember, in most cases this ministry is a process not an event. God uses the process to not only bring deliverance and healing, but to also teach God's people. Be patient but persistent.

Fear is a possible door. Have your friend pray the prayer and complete the checklist. Then ask what fears they checked. Every fear indicates a lack of belief in a biblical truth. In some cases, I will teach a scripture verse to offset a fear. Have them renounce the fears they checked in the appropriate renunciation prayer. Make note of the areas they checked. Just between you and me, there really should not be any fears checked. If there are, this indicates either a lack of biblical knowledge or a demonic foothold and possibly one or more spirits called "fear." I have confronted many spirits called "fear" in people's lives. I have also found that there can be several spirits named "fear" working in a person's life. Sometimes they travel in groups. This is a common spirit to address during the confrontation stage.

We now come to the final **step 7** dealing with family history of sins and curses. If mom, dad, grandmother or grandfather were struggling with footholds in their lives, it's possible the spirits troubling them could actually enter the life of the baby. In my own ministry, this has been a common door for footholds and the devouring of believers. Have your Christian friend pray (aloud) the **Declaration** and then the **Prayer**. Remember to ask if they're hearing anything on the radio.

After they complete the Steps To Freedom, encourage them for the progress they've made. The entire process to this point will normally take around 2-3 hours. In some cases, your friends will not complete these steps in the initial meeting. That's fine. Just schedule another session and continue where you left off. Don't allow your friend to dominate the meeting. You're there to complete the steps. Stay on task. At the same time, be sensitive to their needs.

Chapter Eight

Confronting Demons

Normally, people are apprehensive and somewhat fearful prior to my meeting with them. That's rightly so. I think I would have been nervous also, prior to beginning this ministry. This is an unknown to most people. There's always fear of the unknown.

But by the time you complete the Steps, they are much more relaxed. These steps are good. They will strengthen your friend. Even though these steps are taxing physically and emotionally, our friends will be strengthened spiritually. That's what happens when we do what Scripture says, *"Submit yourselves, therefore, to God" (James 4:7).* These steps really do help to accomplish this spiritual strengthening. But the next few words in James say to then *"resist the devil and he will flee from you."* I do that very literally in this Confrontation Stage. If there are any spirits that are devouring your friend from a foothold position, The Steps to Freedom process weakens them, and this stage removes them.

I will normally take a short break before beginning this stage. My partner has made notes throughout the meeting. These notes will lead us to areas of confrontation. As an example, if my friend checked several boxes in the "fear" section, I will go there first to see if there are any spirits called "fear" or causing fear.

I ask my Christian friend for approval to confront any spirits that may be here. I explain what I'm going to do.

- I tell them, "I'm going to look and speak at you but I will not be speaking to you, but rather to the spirit I'm addressing." People generally understand and agree with this.
- Then I let them know, "If there is a spirit here, the spirit will speak into your mind. The speaking will come to you as thoughts." They've already been listening to these thoughts, in some cases, for most of their lives. I ask them to tell me what they hear or think. In other words, keep the radio on. Some people will actually see things in their mind's eye. Some people will see words or scenes. Just have them explain what they see or hear.

For me, I prefer to be in close proximity to my Christian friend, approximately 4-5 feet away. I begin with prayer. I ask God to not allow any spirits to hide and that we desire healing, deliverance from any and all enemies of the Lord Jesus Christ. I will say, "Let's try it. Are you ready?" Then I begin to confront with the following statement and question.

1st Question:

"I want to know if there are any spirits called fear or causing fear here with a foothold in (person's name) life. Get up here and look at me. You're here because God has you here. I know that and you know that. Now answer my questions and I command the truth from you. You'll only speak into (person's name) mind... Do you understand that you have been defeated by the Lord Jesus Christ on the cross?...Answer me."

Wait a moment and if there is no answer ask your friend, "Did you hear anything?" In some cases people will hear the answer as a thought, but they will think it's just them thinking the thought. I ask them to keep a clear or open mind and tell me what they hear or think. In many cases the people will hear a very clear answer.

Sometimes our friend will hear a "NO" answer from the spirit. That's ok. I normally will answer, *"That's a lie. You <u>are</u> going to tell me the truth. Father, force that spirit to speak the truth. 'Do you understand that you have been defeated by the Lord Jesus Christ on the cross?...answer me with the truth.'"* The spirit will answer, "Yes." They don't like to respond to my authority but they do. I'm establishing or demonstrating my authority over them. Keep in mind that for some of these spirits, this may be the first time the spirits have been confronted directly by someone who knows their authority over them. They've been deceiving people for thousands of years, generation after generation. Now they have run into you. You have authority over them. Don't be shy about using your God-given authority. It's what's going to help your friend that is sitting before you.

2nd Question:
"Do you understand that (<u>person's name</u>) is a child of God and belongs to Jesus Christ, not you?"

They will answer, "Yes." If it's a "No" answer, which I occasionally get, simply reply, *"That's a lie."* Once again, *"I command the truth. Do you understand that (<u>person's name</u>) is a child of God and belongs to Jesus Christ and not you?"* "Yes." Occasionally my Christian friend will hear, "Yes, No, Yes, No." I simply tell the spirit to stop with the 'yes, no' and answer with the truth. They will. Don't give in to these kind of diversionary answers.

3rd Question: (optional)
"What is your purpose in (<u>person's name</u>) life? What have you been assigned to accomplish? I command the truth from you."

Their purpose will give you an idea of their name. Their names usually correspond to what they do in a person's life. It's not necessary to have the names of spirits to remove them. But they work in groups. So that gives me an idea of other possible spirits to find and remove who may be working within that group. Here are some examples I've received from the question *"What is your purpose in (person's name) life? What have you been assigned to accomplish?"* This is only a sample list.

"**To destroy him.**" Based upon this answer this spirit could be named Destruction or Destroy.

"**To kill him.**" This could be a spirit called Death, Destruction, or Kill. I will then answer with, "Is your name Destruction?" "No." "Is your name Death?" "Yes." I like to know their names, but I don't need their name to remove them.

"**To bring depression.**" Could be a spirit called Despair, Depression, Defeat, Hopelessness, Despondency, Hurt or Fear.

"**To confuse him/her.**" Could be a spirit called Confusion, Frustration, Forgetfulness.

"**To bring doubt.**" Could be a spirit called Doubt, Unbelief, Fear, etc. These are only samples.

"**To deceive.**" Could be a spirit called Deception, Delusion, Self-delusion, Pride.

"**To promote jealousy.**" Could be a spirit called Jealousy or Suspicion, or Distrust, or Envy.

"**To bring anger and unforgiveness.**" Could be a spirit called Anger, Bitterness, Hatred, Resentment.

"**To bring immorality to his mind and body.**" Could be a spirit called Immorality, Porn, Pornography, Sensuality, Seduction, Masturbation.

"**To bring indecision.**" Could be a spirit called Confusion, or Indecision, Procrastination, Doubt or Indifference.

I once was talking to another pastor in our city. He shared with me that for quite some time he had been having trouble making decisions. He just couldn't seem to find any comfort in his decision making process. He was being tormented in his mind. I asked him if he wanted to see if that was a spirit that was doing that to him. He hesitantly said, "Yes." We brought another friend and the three of us went to a private room in my church building. I went directly to the confrontation stage.

After prayer, I explained to him what I was going to do. I explained the radio to him. He was to listen for answers from any spirit. I said, "Are you ready?" He nodded yes. *"I want to know what spirit is causing the indecision in this man of God's life. Get up here and look at me, now."* I then asked my first question. *"I command the truth to this question. Do you understand that you have been defeated by the Lord Jesus Christ on the cross?"* He heard loudly in his mind, "YES!" The pastor was very surprised by what he heard. It almost shocked him. Then I asked, *"Do you understand that (person's name) is a child of God and belongs to Jesus and not to you?"* Another loud "Yes." *"Do you have any grounds to remain in his life. I command the truth."* "No." *"Then you leave right now. Go right through that wall and leave our presence...now. Release his mind. Release his emotions. Release your foothold and get out of our presence. (Person's name) doesn't want you. Go where Jesus sends you. You'll never come back. Go! Now! Get out of here!"* That spirit left. The pastor felt him go. We then found and confronted two other spirits and removed them. After this I could find no other footholds. I tried, but the pastor heard nothing more to any of my questioning. He left with a smile on his face.

Sometimes the spirits pretend to leave. I never trust them. I'll ask again, "Is that spirit that I was just talking to still here? If you're still here, we're still talking. You're not hiding from me. Are you still here? Answer me." Sometimes I get a "yes" answer. I then reply, "Why didn't you leave when I told you to go?" They'll say, "I don't want to." or "I don't have to." or "I'm stronger than you." These replies are all lies. I'll tell that spirit, "That's the wrong answer." I then tell them again to go using the same wording. They leave.

Occasionally I'll ask if that spirit is still here and I'll get a "No" answer. Then I want to know who answered me "No?" After I identify that spirit, I'll go back to see if the previous spirit is still here. Once I'm satisfied he is gone I'll address the one who said "No." All this is normally in the Confrontation stage. But if the spirit is bothersome and continually trying to interrupt us during the Steps stage, I'll confront him at that point and remove him. But in most cases, I'll tell the spirit to be quiet, make a note and continue in the Steps.

4ᵗʰ Question:

"Do you have any grounds to remain here in (person's name) life?"

If you get a "yes" answer, ask, "Ok, what grounds do you have?" Let me give you a sample of answers that I have received from various evil spirits after a "yes" response.

With spirits called Fear: *"What grounds do you have?"* The spirit replies, "Because they are fearful." If that's the answer, talk to your friend about this possibility. Then ask your friend to confess this fear and renounce it with scriptural truth. "I renounce fear. God has not given me a spirit of fear, but of power, love and a sound mind. Father, forgive me for my fear and lack of trust in You."

Then go back to the spirit. I normally ask, *"Spirit of Fear, did you hear that?"* "Yes." *"Do you have further grounds?"* "No." Then proceed to command it to leave and remove it.

With spirits called Anger or Bitterness: *"What grounds do you have to remain?"*

The reply might be, "Because they like their anger." Some people hold on to anger and bitterness. They've got to reject that. Confess and renounce all anger and bitterness. Forgive anyone who needs to be forgiven. Remove these grounds.

Then proceed to remove this spirit.

With sexual spirits: *"What grounds do you have to remain?"*

"Because he/she likes what I do." Some people actually like what demons do for them sexually. Until they confess and renounce their sexual sin and the sexual spirits, you won't go far in helping them.

I'm always cautious listening to demons. Their nature is to lie. But I will check with my friend concerning what they say. I have found, in many cases, they actually tell me the truth. But be cautious with information that comes from demons. In many cases, after you complete the Steps To Freedom, you will find that the demons are discouraged and realize they have no grounds to remain.

Now remove the spirit: *"I command you, spirit of Fear, to leave (person's name). I command you to go right through that wall (as I point to an exterior wall) and leave our presence. Go! Now! Release (person's name) mind.*
Release (person's name) emotions.
And release your foothold that you've had in (person's name) life. Your work is over here. You go where Jesus sends you. You're not staying. Get out now. Release him/her. You're never coming back. Get out of here...now!"

This type of command usually removes the spirit. Ask your friend what happened, or what went on while you were speaking. Ask them if that spirit left. Sometimes they will know. Sometimes they won't. Sometimes they feel it go. Sometimes the spirit says, "Ok, I'm leaving." Don't trust their words. Check to make sure they left. I'll say, *"Spirit of Fear, are you still here? If you're still here we're still talking. You're not tricking me. Are you still here? Answer me."* If they're still there they will answer. I will then ask them,

"Why didn't you go when I told you to go?" Normally I hear, "I don't won't to." I answer, *"But you are leaving."* Sometimes they will tell me, "I'm strong." I just pull out the sword of the Spirit and quote, *"Greater is He who is in me that he who is in the world"* (1 *John 4:4*). Now repeat the removal command. They normally go.

Occasionally those I'm meeting with will actually see the spirit leave. Do I ever see them leave? No. I never have. In Seminary one day I was talking to a pastor who asked me to come and meet with a man named Jim. He had not been able to help Jim. The three of us met together. The pastor was somewhat skeptical and unsure of this process. During the confrontation stage I confronted the first spirit. Upon removing him with the above commands, the pastor said, "Dave, did you see that?" His eyes were shocked and wide open. I said, "See what?" He replied, "I just saw that spirit leave Jim and go right past us and out of the room." Jim felt him leave also. I think the Lord allowed the pastor to see this to let him know that this really happened. It's real. And it's a great aid to the saints.

One evening I received a phone call from a friend. His daughter was struggling with what he thought might be a spirit. The spirit was manifesting in their presence. I asked if I could be put on the speaker phone. Upon addressing the spirit I eventually commanded it to go. I had the father point to an exterior wall and told the spirit to go right through that wall. Even through using the speaker phone several spirits were removed. His daughter said she counted 9 spirits leave. They looked like shadows to her. While some people can see a visual image of them, most do not.

Now talk with your partner and see where their notes indicate any further area for confrontation. Normally, I will check to see if there are any other spirits called Fear or other spirits who are working with the spirit of Fear. I will say something like, *"I want to know if there are any other spirits called Fear here. I command your presence before me. Look at me. Answer my questions truthfully. 'Do you understand that you have been defeated by the Lord Jesus Christ on the cross?...Answer me.'"* If you receive a "yes" answer continue to use your authority over that spirit and remove him. If there is no response, or no answer, it may mean there are no other spirits called fear there.

Your partner should be taking notes and recording what's happening. Always record the name of the spirit you are addressing or what the spirit has been sent to accomplish. Keep finding and removing these spirits.

I will present the question, "Where do we go next?" to all three of us sitting there. We talk freely among us. You are a team, all three of you. After looking at the notes you may decide to see what spirit caused that headache about two hours ago.

"I want to know what spirit caused that headache awhile back? Get up here and get before me. You're here because God's got you here. Answer my question. I command the truth from you. Do you understand that you have been disarmed by Jesus Christ who made a public display of you having triumphed over you? Answer me." "Yes." *"And do you understand that (friend's name) belongs to the Lord Jesus Christ?"* "Yes." I think, in this case, I would like to know the name of this spirit. So I would ask, *"What's your purpose in (friends name) life?* "To bring pain to her life." *"Is your name Pain?"* If they tell me "No," you can ask what his name is. Sometimes I receive an answer, sometimes I don't. But often I will say, *"Well, I'm going to call you the spirit who causes pain, whether that's your name or not." "Do you have any grounds to remain in (person's name) life?"* "No." *"Then I command you, spirit I'm calling Pain, to leave (person's name). I command you to go right through that wall* (as I point to an exterior wall) *and leave our presence. Go! Now!*
Release (person's name) mind.
Release (person's name) emotions.
And release your foothold on his/her body.
Your work here is over. You go where Jesus sends you. You're not

staying. Get out now. Release this man/woman of God. You're never coming back. Get out of here...now!"

I will then ask the individual, "Did that spirit leave?" I never trust them. Check and see if they are still there. I say, *"If you're still here, the spirit I was just talking to, we're still talking. Are you still here? Answer me."* If we receive a "Yes" answer, I'll ask the spirit, just as before, *"Why didn't you go when I just told you to go?"* Normally they will give me an answer like, "Because I don't want to, or I don't have to, or I'm stronger than you." None of that is true. I simply reply, *"Yes, you do have to leave"* or *"Greater is He who is in me than you who are in the world."* Then I begin, once again, my commands to remove that spirit. Almost always they go after completing round two.

If after two or three rounds they are still there and haven't left yet, there must be a reason. Find the reason. In this case there is always a "key" to be discovered. Find the "key." There may be a sin that needs to be confessed. There could be a **curse** that needs to be broken. Here are some possible origins of a curse.

1. Curses can come from a practitioner, a person placing a curse on an individual or family.

I once met with Janice, a missionary from Africa. She explained to me that for years she was depressed. She couldn't read her Bible or even pray. She also told me she would only be here for two days. I met with her and, with her permission, five other ladies that I was training. We went through the Steps To Freedom. It took much longer than I thought it would. We stopped for the day. I told her to call me in the morning and let me know how she did during the night. She called the next morning and said she had nightmares all night long. I called her back for our second meeting with all the trainees in attendance.

I went to the confrontation stage and began like this. *"I want to know who was causing the nightmares last night? Get up here. I command your presence before me and I command the* truth from you. Do you understand you were defeated by the Lord Jesus Christ on the cross?" The spirit answered, "Yes." I asked, "How long have you been working in this woman of God's life?" The spirit answered, "Four years." I then asked the missionary if that answer make any sense. She said that it did. I asked her what happened four years ago. She said her husband had purchased a plot of land. The worker on the land had to be removed because it was now their land. But it just so happened that he was a shaman, a witch doctor. She told me he put a round ball of something on their fence post. They thought it might be a curse, but they really didn't put too much stock in curses. But from that point, things began to crumble in her life and in other members of her family. I said, "I break this curse in the name and authority of Jesus Christ. It will no longer stand in effect in this family." I had her renounce the curse and break its bond in her life and family.

I then addressed that spirit again. "Do you have any grounds, presently, to remain in Janice's life?" The spirit said, "No." I then said, "Are you ready to leave?" The spirit answered, "We have to." I like it when I hear that kind of answer. I said, "Ok, all of you go, now. Leave this woman and her family, now. It's over. Get out. You'll never return." She said, "They're gone!!" She smiled. She couldn't stop smiling. She said she hasn't been able to smile for four years. Then she began to laugh. It was like she couldn't stop laughing. She apologized for laughing. She hadn't laughed for four years. I said for her to keep right on laughing. I left her and the ladies to rejoice together. What a wonderful healing the Lord did there in our midst.

Curses are serious and can have devastating effects. I'm always alert to the possibility of a curse that may need to be broken during my meetings. I'm always alert to the possibility of a curse coming against me and my family. If I suspect something strange, I break it and command any enemies of the Lord Jesus Christ to leave my presence. What if it's not a curse? Great. No problem then. I'd rather address it and it be no issue than not address it and it actually be a curse.

2. Curses can be made unknowingly by certain statements made to an individual, usually by an authority figure (parents, doctors, pastors, even friends). What kind of statements? "You'll never amount to anything in your life." "You're always going to be stupid." "You're lazy and will never change." "You'll have this disease for the rest of your life." "You'll always be an alcoholic." Demons can actually take advantage of these kinds of statements.

One day I was meeting with a very bright young lady from our church. We were looking for a "key" for removing an enemy spirit who was assaulting her and accusing her. We explored the possibility of a verbal curse. I asked her if she remembered anyone in her past who used any of these types of statements toward her. She said her father would often make those kind of statements to her. I had her renounce those statements as lies. We broke any curse that may have resulted from those awful statements. *"We break and cancel any curse that you enemies may have used to take advantage of (person's name). We break every bond resulting from those curses."* After this, it was easy to remove the spirits that had gained a place in her life as a result of those kinds of statements made by her father.

3. Curses can come through our ancestors. These are also known as blood-line curses.

One day I received a call from a 19 year old girl named Carol, who also attended our church. She was experiencing many physical problems. Doctors could not find a cure for her many ailments. She showed me a list of her physical issues which included chronic fatigue, migraines, irritable bowel syndrome and lactose intolerance. Then she showed me a list of her medications she was presently on. This list filled an 8 ½ x 11 sheet of paper. She wanted to know if the issues in her life had any spiritual root. She needed help. I answered, "Do you want to meet and begin to explore the possibility?" She said, without hesitation, "Yes!" Carol and her parents were excited about this new possibility.

During the course of our meetings, we broke several blood-line curses passed down to this young girl from her ancestry. We broke the bond, or connection these spirits had with her and removed many spirits during the course of many months. She was tenacious and so were we.

One day she showed up for another confrontation meeting and Carol showed us the list of meds she was taking. Let me say here and now, I never tell a person I'm meeting with to stop their medications prescribed by their doctor. That's not my job and certainly not within the scope of any pastor's position. She told us, during the course of several months, as she was experiencing more healing, that she had stopped her meds, all except one. She said her doctor was helping her off her last medication. She was under the care of her doctor. I was relieved to hear that her doctor was working with her. After many months Carol was healed from all her diseases.

Earlier she had told us she decided to see if her lactose intolerance was still present. So she ate a bowl of ice cream to see what would happen. Nothing happened. She now could eat anything she wanted. The migraines were gone. The chronic fatigue was gone. All her other physical issues were healed. The glory goes to God. But God very often works through His people. In this case, my partner and me. How did all this happen? It happened through submission, resisting the devil, and prayer.

1) Helping Carol to submit to God and resist the devil.

By using our authority to break curses and remove demonic footholds, thereby stopping their devouring. Carol was very much involved in her own healing. These spirits were actively causing physical issues in Carol's body.

2) Surround this whole process with prayer.

We always include prayer ministry with our deliverance ministry. My partner and I prayed each meeting for Carol's healing. We prayed for her spiritual, emotional and physical healing. Over the course of these meetings, several times, I anointed Carol with oil and my partner and I prayed for her. We spoke to the mountain of issues in her life and told them they were finished. We commanded that mountain to leave her and depart from her into the sea (Matthew 21:21). And they did.

Remember, it's God who works through each of us. If *He is able to do exceedingly, abundantly above all that we ask or think, according to the power that works in us (Ephesians 3:20),* then let's ask big, with child-like faith.

We removed, possibly, 100 demonic footholds from the life of this young lady. I can hear your question. Could there actually be that many spirits sent against a young girl? Let me answer this way. Jesus removed seven spirits from Mary Magdalene (Mark 16:9). At one point Jesus crossed the Sea of Galilee and met a man. He perhaps cast a few thousand spirits (Legion) out of him (Mark 5)! In this ministry, we will meet dear people that need our help. Devouring may be actively taking place through spirits numbering anywhere from a few to "legion". Most of the people I've met with have had in the range of 4 to 50.

Remember, the spirits can only attack the body and soul (mind, emotions and will) of a believer. They cannot touch your spirit. Your spirit is born again. But they do attempt to hassle our sinful flesh, thus, the warning in Scripture.

So curses can come from various sources. 1) From people who purpose to put curses on others. 2) From people who unknowingly put verbal curses on others. 3) Curses that come from the sins of our ancestors.

Evil spirits work in groups. I'll normally stay and attempt to remove all the spirits in a group before I move to another group. For example, evil spirits causing headaches are most likely in a different group from those causing fear or depression. I have found spirits called Fear in different groups in a person's life. So if you remove a particular spirit that you know the name of, you could also find, at a later date, another spirit with the same name.

It's not that they came back, it's simply that there can be multiple spirits with the same name having different footholds in a person's life.

I hope I've given you a good foundation to begin a deliverance ministry. If you believe God is leading you to join with me in helping free our brothers and sisters in Christ, you will need copies of *The Steps To Freedom In Christ,* Neil T. Anderson. 1-800-4-GOSPEL, or www.gospellight.com, or find them on Amazon.

Of course there are many other possible issues that may arise during the course of your meetings. Let's talk about some these in the next chapter.

Chapter Nine

Other Deliverance Ministry Issues

U sually there is a *normal* in the deliverance ministry process. But you will also find the "not normal" in this ministry. Let's look at some other related topics, and also some of the "not normal" issues.

Subsequent meetings

I always schedule a second and third meeting with each person I meet with. Normally, I wait a week before our next meeting, but in some cases I will meet sooner. This depends upon their need and your time constraints. Their homework is to journal their spiritual experiences, particularly where they had victories and where they were hit with temptation, accusation or deception. We'll review their notes as we begin the next meeting. The follow-up appointments are confrontation based. Our goal is to remove all demonic footholds from their life, so keep scheduling appointments until all footholds are gone. How will you know? You will find no further footholds in their life. Also, they will have healing and relief from what was plaguing them.

Meetings with wrong motives

I have met with several men and women over the years where the meetings seem to accomplish much. Spirits are confronted and removed. But over the weeks, little to no ground is gained in their life. When this happens, there's usually one common thread in these meetings. The person is there with wrong motives. Some just want the attention. Some come to gain approval with their spouse. One lady came because her mother made her. These kinds of meetings may seem to go well, or not, but produce no fruit. I must admit, I often cannot tell when a person comes with wrong motives. But it happens. Ask God to reveal to you or your partner whatever you need to know to help the friend that's come to you.

Derailing roadblocks

I once was meeting with a woman who was dealing with various foothold issues in her life. They were strong spirits that actually took hold of her behavior. Her demeanor would change right before me. Her language would change. One of her issues was stealing, and one of the spirits I dealt with was called Robber. Her husband didn't know she had this problem. She was lying to him and deceiving him, and so we were not progressing. We came to a point in our meetings when I asked her to confess to her husband and share with him this issue she was dealing with. He needed to know, but she refused to cooperate. I could go no further with her deliverance. I wondered why the spirits were so strong and had such control of her life. At that point I knew. When people are before you and want freedom, but will not submit to God's Word, it will greatly hinder, but most likely stop the deliverance process.

Physical rather than spiritual

There are physical issues that very much look like demonic manifestation but are not. Both men and women can come to you with symptoms that sound like enemy footholds.

I always explore possible physical causes such as hormonal imbalance, and ask if they are currently under any medical care.

Many years ago, Sue was having an anger issue toward her husband and children. After quite some time, she looked at a possible hormonal imbalance and began medical treatment. It completely eliminated the anger issue. But in other cases there may be a physical issue combined with demonic activity. Ask her to see her doctor. But continue the healing and deliverance ministry with her. Our ministry is to "help" our Christian friends and neighbors.

Nonsense answers

When in the confrontation stage, I'll confront a spirit asking, *"Do you understand that you have been defeated by the Lord Jesus Christ?"* Sometimes the answer will come like this, "Yes, no, yes, no, yes, no." Demons don't like to submit to my authority and answer my questions. But they have to. So sometimes the answer will be nonsense. I'll tell them to stop those kinds of answers and give me the truth. Sometimes I'll ask the Holy Spirit to surround that spirit. The Holy Spirit is also known as the Spirit of Truth. Then I'll ask the question once again and they will often stop the nonsense and answer correctly.

Deceiving demon tactics

Occasionally, in the confrontation stage, you will go through the process of removing a spirit and it will appear to have left. The person may even feel a release and/or a peace. But I don't trust the deceiving spirit. Often I'll tell my friend that I'm going to check and see if that spirit actually left. I'll say, "I want to know if that spirit I just confronted is still here. If you're still here, we're still talking. You're not going to hide on me. Get up here if you're still here. Now reveal yourself to me. Are you still here?" Sometimes your friend will hear the answer, "No." The question then becomes, "Who said 'no'"? It could be that there is a second spirit, a lesser one, that is trying to divert me from confronting the

spirit, a lesser one, that is trying to divert me from confronting the first spirit. If this happens, I'll address the spirit who said "no." It's almost always a different spirit. I will then tell that spirit to go down and wait. Then I go back to my original course of action. Occasionally, that spirit I first commanded to go only pretended to go and was hiding. I address him again and remove him. Then I'll go back and address the one who said "no" and remove that lesser spirit.

Our motive in this ministry

If you decide to enter this ministry, your motive must never be to man-handle demons or to order evil spirits around. Our motive is always to bring glory to God by loving and helping His people. I want to be involved in rescuing the devoured because it's part of making disciples. We work through a humble spirit, but with powerful authority.

Our mindset in this ministry

One day Jesus sent 70 disciples out to preach, heal and cast out demons. They came back very excited, but Jesus reminded them of their even greater blessing.

> 17 *"The seventy returned with joy, saying, "Lord, even the demons are subject to us in Your name." 18 And Jesus said to them, "I was watching Satan fall from heaven like lightning. 19 "Behold, I have given you authority to tread on serpents and scorpions, and over all the power of the enemy, and nothing will injure you. 20 Nevertheless do not rejoice in this, that the spirits are subject to you, but rejoice that your names are recorded in heaven: (Luke 10:17-20).*

The use of oil

In some cases, a particular spirit you are dealing with may be stronger than normal and difficult to remove. Sometimes I will anoint the person with oil. I explain this oil, in Scripture, represents the Holy Spirit and healing. It's also used to set apart servants as holy unto the Lord. I normally will put oil on my finger and apply it to the forehead with the following statement. *"Sally, I anoint you with this oil in the name of the Father, Son and Holy Spirit."* I make the sign of the cross on the forehead. I'll then have my partner and I place our hands on the person's head or shoulder. I always ask first if it's ok for me to place my hand on a lady's shoulder. Then we proceed to command the spirit to leave.

Teaching your friend their own authority

Occasionally, possibly in the second or third meeting, I'll ask our Christian friend to become involved in commanding a particular spirit to leave them. Some are more adept at this than others. Use your good judgment here. But it's exciting when they learn that they actually have authority over these spirits themselves.

Healing/prayer ministry

Healing/prayer ministry goes hand-in-hand with deliverance ministry. It's certainly worth devoting the next chapter to.

Chapter Ten

Healing/Prayer Ministry[8]

The purpose of this chapter is not to give you biblical proof that God still heals today. You already believe that physical healing is one of the works Jesus said those who believe in Him would do. *Truly, truly, I say to you, he who believes in Me, the works that I do, he will do also; (John 14:12a).* I include this chapter to give you a framework for pursuing informal or formal ministry in prayer leading to healing. Rescuing the devoured and healing are under the same umbrella. The steps are given to help people learn to crawl and walk and run. This information will aid your deliverance ministry. It will be of great use in praying for the healing of your friends. Things to remember:

- The steps below are NOT the formula for healing. This is an exercise to help grow in this ministry. You can't find a formula in Scripture. Jesus healed in many different ways.
- The steps mentioned are not exhaustive. Many other issues could be in play.
  - Sometimes God wants the person to take time to deal with sin issues.
  - Sometimes our little faith is in play.
  - Sometimes the issue may be demons causing physical issues.
  - Sometimes the Holy Spirit uses people in more

unique ways than others, etc. Such as the spiritual gifts of healings.

- Sometimes God is working another purpose.

All deliverance and healing should be done in response to what the Father wants done. Jesus is our example. He only did what the Father desired. Obviously we are not Jesus. We have desires. In most cases, our desire is healing for our friend. That's normally our default position. But remember, God may have another desire.

I believe God probably wants more people healed than we have believed in the past. So try. God works through people. God manifests spiritual gifts and His authority through church people for the common good and for His glory.

Throughout these steps, always have your ears open to the Lord for what He wants to do. His way is the right way and probably the easier way. Most of us are not used to listening for the Holy Spirit. Can the Holy Spirit speak to us today? Acts 21:11 Concerning a man named Agabus: *"Coming over to us, he took Paul's belt, tied his own hands and feet with it and said, 'The Holy Spirit says, In this way the Jews of Jerusalem will bind the owner of this belt...'"* Certainly. God the Spirit can do whatever He desires. So don't let these steps be a hindrance! These are an offering to help you.

Be aware of what the Holy Spirit is doing in you through the process. Often the focus is on the issues of the person seeking healing, but the Holy Spirit may want to reveal issues in you as well.

Healing Ministry Steps:

Step 1: Interview – "What's going on? What hurts? What's wrong?"

Listen to them: Filter what you hear through Biblical knowledge and previous experiences. If you are doing deliverance ministry all these issues will come to light during the interview.

Listen to the Lord. He may give further information for helping the person. Caution: It can be easy to forget the Holy Spirit and trust our own experience.

We don't need extensive medical information like a doctor would. This interview can be quick and to the point – don't delay the healing.

Step 2: Diagnosis – "Why is this condition present?"

Natural? (Dislocated shoulder playing sports, etc.)

Sin issue? (Sickness directly related to sin in the life – 1 Cor. 11:28-30; James 5). When people call for the elders of the church to pray for their healing, the Scripture says they are to confess their sins one to another. Why? Because sin may be the cause of the physical issue. Deal with the sin first, then prayer for healing.

Emotional issue? (Anxiety, fear, etc.)

Relational issue? (Lack of forgiveness, anger, resentment, hatred, etc.) A lady came for prayer during the closing worship songs. She was having stomach pains. After prayer there was no healing. The ladies praying for her asked her if there were any forgiveness issues in her life. She said, "Yes." They led her to forgive those she was holding anger and bitterness toward. They prayed again. She was healed.

Demonic issue? Demons can use any of the above issues to bring about sickness. In some New Testament examples people submitted to Jesus for healing and He cast out demons to bring about the healing. Some examples:

Matthew 12:22 – Man blind and mute

Matthew 17:14-18 – Boy with seizures

Luke 13:10-13 – Woman bent over for 18 years

Curses? Some sicknesses do not come from a person's own issues but from other people; such as abuse, curses, oaths, or sins of our ancestors. We need to engage in this battle.

Let's review our information on Curses.

Curses can come purposefully; such as from witchdoctors, black magic, or people practicing curses through their willful involvement with demons.

Curses can come through people ignorantly; such as through Masonic vows. Blood-line curses can come unintentionally through the sins of ancestors.

Curses can also come from comments like, "I hate you." "I wish you were never born." "You'll never amount to anything." Or through authoritative announcements; such as from a pastor or a doctor declaring, "You'll always live with this." "This is chronic illness."

Sometimes the diagnosis is a combination of any of the situations listed above. For example, if someone seeks healing for migraines, the diagnosis might be any of the those listed above.

Often, the person seeking healing will not know the diagnosis and will not link a disorder to a potential spiritual source. So it could be necessary for you to gently and humbly ask the correct questions and seek the counsel of the Holy Spirit.

- How long has this being going on?
- Has your walk with Jesus been consistent?
- How are you doing right now with forgiveness, anxiety, fear? Etc.

Remember: the root causes of sicknesses come from beyond the natural realm more than we would think; but the easiest approach to your diagnosis is to remain in the natural realm. This is OK – but take time to discern and don't be afraid to re-address your diagnosis if healing hasn't happened.

Step 3: Choose your healing prayer/command – Do the healing

Remember:

- Jesus has given us authority – use it. This is the same authority He has given to us over demons.
- We operate in various levels of faith – grow in it. In any area of ministry our faith will grow as we minister in that area over a period of time.
- We operate in various areas of power and giftedness – ask for it.
- We don't see people in the New Testament asking God to heal others, or asking God to remove demons; we see them using their God-given authority to remove demons and to heal others...to command both demons and healing. This is an area of debate in the church. But I believe we can speak to the mountain (of illness, etc.) and tell it, command it, to

move and be cast into the sea just as we command demons to leave. In other words, can the same authority that we use to remove demons be used on sickness and physical issues? Yes. I do both. I address my Father, "God, you know our hearts. We desire healing." Then, I command healing with my God-given authority. Peter did the same when he was asked to go to Joppa. A lady named Dorcus had died. When Peter arrived this is what he did. *Peter knelt down and prayed, and turning to the body, he said, "Tabitha, arise." And she opened her eyes (Acts 9:40).* Peter knelt and prayed first. Then he turned to the body and commanded her to rise. Jesus said we would do the same deeds He did (Jn. 14:12). He also said to proclaim the gospel of the kingdom, cast out demons and heal the sick. These are things *we* have the authority to do. Of course, the results are all through the power of God and for His glory. *Now to Him who is able to do far more abundantly beyond all that we ask or think, **according to the power that works within us, to Him be the glory**...(Ephesians 3:20-21).*

- We don't see people healing in the New Testament using many words. We often use many words because we are just not sure what else to do. This is a sign that waiting on the Lord is a devalued part of the process.

Some have suggested that by using our authority through commands, such as, "I command this elbow to be healed in the name of Jesus," we are actually commanding God to do it. Therefore, they find this command prayer very uncomfortable. If that were the case, I would certainly agree. But when we use commands to remove demons or heal the sick, we aren't commanding God. We're simply using our God-given authority to do what He told us to do - heal the sick and cast out demons.

In healing it may feel we're commanding God because we have been asking God to heal others all our Christian lives. Our prayers for healing have always been directed to God. So when we use our God-given authority we may still see ourselves directing our words to God. In reality, we're directing our words to demons or sickness. We are not commanding God when we use the authority he delegated to us. We're privileged to do what God has authorized us to do.

He has given to us authority (ability, the right) to cast out demons, heal the sick and preach the gospel. It's part of being a child of God. This authority, or this "right", comes to each believer when we receive the Holy Spirit.

> *John 1:12*
> *12 But as many as received Him, to them He gave the* **right** *to become children of God, even to those who believe in His name.*

The word "right" (exousia) is also translated as *authority* and *power*. God has given to everyone who has received Jesus authority and power. I believe there's more than just a position referred to here, but the ability to act and to exercise the authority of God. Jesus refers to this authority.

> *John 14:12*
> *"Truly, truly, I say to you, he who believes in Me, the works that I do, he will do also; and greater works than these he will do; because I go to the Father.*

How is it that we can do these authoritative works? Look at the last six words; *"because I go to the Father."* After Jesus went to the Father, Jesus sent the Holy Spirit into every believer's life. It was by the power of the Holy Spirit that Jesus did His works. It's the same Holy Spirit that accomplishes the same works through our lives... *the works that I do, he will do also.* But those works will not happen if we do not use His delegated authority. Jesus explains what He did for the twelve.

> *Luke 9:1-2*
> *And He called the twelve together, and gave them power and authority over all the demons and to heal diseases. 2 And He sent them out to proclaim the kingdom of God and to perform healing.*

The twelve in this text performed healings by Jesus' delegated authority. The word for "authority" is the same word for "right" in John 1:12. They were given authority over demons and authority to heal diseases. They didn't ask God to heal the diseases. They *performed* the healings. This is the way God operated in the first century. They healed using their delegated authority and power. This is why we don't see the believers in the Bible asking God to heal, as is our practice today. Allow me to clarify here. It's important to understand that the power for deliverance and healing always comes from God. And He has granted us the privilege to deliver the package (gift).

I also believe Luke 9:1-2 has a degree of transfer to us today. Since Jesus has "all authority in heaven and **on earth**," He told us to go into the world and make disciples. That included teaching everyone what Jesus taught them. Jesus certainly taught them about casting out demons and healing the sick. (Jesus said that whoever believes *"will lay hands on the sick, and they will recover." (Mark 16:17-18).*

Jesus also appointed seventy other people to go out and proclaim the kingdom of God. They were also commanded to heal the sick and cast out demons.

> *Luke 10:17-20*
> *17 The seventy returned with joy, saying, "Lord, even*

the demons are subject to us in Your name." 18 And He said to them, "I was watching Satan fall from heaven like lightning. 19 Behold, I have given you authority to tread on serpents and scorpions, and over all the power of the enemy, and nothing will injure you. 20 Nevertheless do not rejoice in this, that the spirits are subject to you, but rejoice that your names are recorded in heaven."

Let me say a few words about man's role vs. God's role.

- Although God can reveal His love for any person without the aid of man, He has ordained that man reveal God's love by loving one another.
- Although God can save any person without the aid of man, He has ordained that man proclaim the gospel for man's salvation. Faith comes by hearing (Romans 10:17).
- Although God can meet anyone's personal needs without the person praying, He has ordained that man ask Him in prayer for their needs (James 4:2-3).
- Although God can teach any person without the aid of man, He has ordained that man teach other men.
- Although God can deliver any person from demons without the aid of man, He has ordained that man cast out demons.
- Although God can heal any person physically without the aid of man, He has ordained that man be involved in healing the sick.

How necessary is faith in healing?

Faith certainly plays a part in healing as we see in Scripture. Whose faith? 1) Faith of the one praying; or 2) Faith of the one needing healing; or 3) Faith of others. Here are examples of each.

1. Faith of the one praying

Matthew 17:19-20
19...“Why could we not drive it out?” 20 “Because of the littleness of your faith; If you have the faith the size of a mustard seed, you will say to this mountain, ‘Move from here to there,’ and it will move; and nothing will be impossible to you”

Matthew 21:21
And Jesus answered and said to them, "Truly I say to you, if you have faith and do not doubt, you will not only do what was done to the fig tree, but even if you say to this mountain, 'Be taken up and cast into the sea,' it will happen.

Luke 17:6
And the Lord said, "If you had faith like a mustard seed, you would say to this mulberry tree, 'Be uprooted and be planted in the sea'; and it would obey you.

In Nazareth unbelief affected the amount of miracles
Mark 6:5-6
5 And He could do no miracle there except that He laid His hands on a few sick people and healed them. 6 And He wondered at the unbelief.

2. Faith of the one needing healing:

Woman sick for 12 years
“If I just touch His garments, I will get well” (Mark 5:28).

“And Jesus said to her, ‘Daughter, your faith has made you well’” (34).

Two blind men

> *28 Jesus said to them, "Do you believe that I am able to do this?" They said to Him, "Yes, Lord." 29 Then He touched their eyes, saying, "It shall be done to you according to your faith" (Matthew 9:28-29).*

Blind man

> *"Rabboni, I want to regain my sight!" 52 And Jesus said to him, "Go; your faith has made you well" (Mark 10:51-52).*

One of 10 Samaritans cleansed from leprosy

> *"Stand up and go; your faith has made you well" (Luke 17:19).*

3. Faith of others concerning healing:

Roman centurion for his servant:

> *"just say the word and my servant will be healed." "I have not found such great faith with anyone in Israel" (Matthew 8:8,10)*

Jesus told the synagogue official whose daughter died:

> *Do not be afraid any longer, only believe" (Mark 5:36)*

Gentile woman with sick daughter

> *"even the dogs feed on the crumbs which fall from their masters' table." 28 Then Jesus said to her, "O woman, your faith is great; it shall be done for you as you wish." And her daughter was healed at once (Matthew 15:27-28).*

Here are some suggestions:

- Posture – invite the person to be in a posture of receiving. The person's natural posture may reveal where their heart is. For example, some postures reveal nervousness, others reveal defeat.

- Anointing with oil — Jesus told the disciples (Mark 6:13) and the church (James 5:14) to use oil. Why? It represents the Holy Spirit. It pictures the presence of the Holy Spirit on the person. It represents healing and the fact that the person is set apart, chosen by God and is His child.
- Talk about the diagnosis — Lead the person to forgive, confess, renounce if applicable, etc.
- Laying on of hands — This is the way Jesus has set up this ministry. Lay hands where the sickness is, if appropriate. (Matthew 19:13; Mark 5:23; 16:18; Acts 9:12; Acts 28:8)
- Invite the powerful presence of God (Holy Spirit) to minister to the person.
- Speak to God, such as... *"Lord, we're seeking healing here. Thank You for the privilege."*
- Command healing in the name of Jesus.
  "I command this elbow to be healed in the name of Jesus."
  "I speak to this mountain (migraine) to be removed, to leave, be cast into the sea."
  "In the name of Jesus, I command the inflammation in Joe's knee to be healed, and all swelling and pain to leave now."
- Break off the power of an afflicting spirit. Suggested type of prayer:
  "If there's an enemy of the Lord Jesus Christ here associated with this sickness, I command that you to stop and leave this person now. Release their mind, their emotions and their body. Go where Jesus sends you. Right now, leave this room."
- Ask the person not to pray, but to focus on the issue...the radio. It's time for them to receive.
- Let your words be few. Luke 7:8 — True authority does not need many words. Using few words is a way to grow in

faith.

- Not only learn to pray few words, but learn to receive few words prayed over you.
  "Open your eyes"
  "Stand up and go; your faith has made you well"
  (Luke 17:19)
  "Stand upright on your feet" (Acts 14:10).
  "In the name of Jesus Christ the Nazarene - walk"
  (Acts 3:6);
  "Go to Siloam and wash" (John 9:11)

  Sometimes people pray long and with eloquence over a person so they can feel like they received a valuable prayer.
- Let your words and actions be free from anything sensational to demonstrate that the power is not in sensational actions.

Step 4: Waiting and Watching – "How are we doing?"

This step is waiting and asking what's happening. Ask the person to communicate everything they are feeling …. Radio on. Has the pain lessened? Is it more? Has it moved? How are you feeling? If the pain is moving, or new pains are coming, it could be a demonic attack. Are there sensations such as (trembling, weeping, weakness, heat, tingling, dizziness, deep breathing, electric feeling, peace, laughter, moaning, rocking back and forth). These are probably signs the Lord is at work. Keep waiting.

If nothing is happening, wait. The Lord can take His time. Many unseen things are at work. People vary in their receptivity to God's working. Some may be rejecting the way the Lord wants to work. Teach yourself to endure this step. This is where you'll be tempted to quit. If nothing immediate happens, you'll be prone to give up. Don't give up! Don't be afraid to receive news. Don't be afraid of being a fool. Don't be afraid of failing. Command healing a second time (Mark 8:22-26).

Do not correct or try to build the person's faith. Their faith may indeed be weak, but it is never helpful to correct it in this moment. You can't "muster up" faith in that moment. You don't need to say things like, "I believe you are going to be healed." You don't know for sure they will be healed. You can have great faith and still not know if they are going to be healed. Saying those words does not "increase the likelihood" of healing and does not create more faith. Stay away from those kind of statements. This is why we need to be like Jesus and do what we see the Father doing. Jesus only knew what the Father revealed to Him – that includes healing ministry.

Many people believe in healing, but not for themselves. We have a prayer team that prays before each Sunday morning church service from 9:00 to 10:00 am. One morning we asked the Lord if there was any prayer direction He wanted us to pray for. One of our young men said to me, "Dave, I think I received this from the Lord. There's someone today who has an elbow issue." Since I was preaching that morning, at the end of my message I got bold, stepped out and said, "If there's someone here that needs prayer, come over to the side and let's pray. It may be something like an elbow issue." A man named Rick came to me and said he's the elbow. He said, "I wasn't going to ask for prayer. He's done so much for me already, but since you mentioned, 'It could even be an elbow,' I'm here." We went to the prayer room. His elbow had been sore and stiff and bent for months. He couldn't even shake hands, it was so painful. He also told me he was going to the doctor the next day. I anointed his elbow with oil and put my hands on the elbow. I told him to let me know how he's feeling. I then said, "Lord, we desire healing for Rick. You know our hearts." I then spoke to the mountain of pain and injury to be gone and cast into the sea. I used my God-given authority and commanded his elbow to be healed in my normal voice. We then waited. My hand was still on his elbow. After ten or twenty seconds, I was going to ask him what was going on and how it felt. But before I got the words out he began to move his arm at the elbow. And then he began to move violently. He was moving it up and down quickly. I thought he would hurt it. It was totally healed. Tears were falling down his face and he shook and squeezed my hand. We laughed. All for God's glory, not man's.

It's Ok to promote a lighthearted atmosphere. The power is not in being hyper-spiritual, nor speaking loudly or eloquently, nor acting flamboyantly. The power rests in authority and faith. Individual gifting can also come into play, but authority and faith are given to every believer.

What do I do if nothing happens?
- Reconsider the diagnosis.
- Continue in a posture of waiting (if you are able).
- If you are out of time, move on to step 5.

Step 5: Post-prayer direction – "How do I keep my healing?" or "How can I pursue my healing?"
- It's possible that healing/deliverance is a process and the process has begun. Continue in an attitude of prayer even as you leave.
- It's possible to be healed and then to be attacked later with the same problem. Command it to go away again. Don't give up and accept it.
- If sin was involved, say as Jesus said, *"Go and sin no more."* Stop the practice of that sin.
- Testify to others if you were healed.
- If you were not healed, keep at it. Pray next week also. Don't give up.

I've written this book as a foundation to help your believing friends, or even seekers, who need spiritual help. A healing or deliverance can go a long way in the life of a believer who may have been brought to you, or in one whom God is drawing to himself.

When someone comes to me for help, I let them know I believe it's a good thing if their troubles are rooted in the spiritual realm. In most cases there's healing and victory there. If their desire is to submit themselves to God and resist the devil, then we will make progress. There's freedom possible if it's a demonic issue. If it's demonic, that's good news for me. I want them to join me in that optimism.

You can help others gain freedom from foothold issues in their lives. It's not a spiritual gift issue, it's the Holy Spirit in you. Your faith puts your authority over spirits into action. Faith without works is dead faith. There's only one way to really learn, and that's by doing. You learn to drive a car by driving, not just by reading a manual. Use the steps and helps I've laid out for you. Don't be afraid. This is where God shows up. He will use you and help you. One pastor said, "Faith is spelled R-I-S-K."[9]

One of the qualities we all will need in this ministry is tenaciousness. Don't give up. They need your ministry. There will be disappointments, but there will also be wonderful healings and freedom gained by many.

There are multitudes out there who believe in Jesus, but many doorways for evil spirits were opened in their past. They are struggling in one or more areas. There are marriages going down for the count. They need help. They need freedom from various levels of demonic devouring. You can bring them that freedom and healing.

I ask God's blessing upon your life as you consider becoming a mango tree. May your passion for Jesus grow. At the same time, may your passion for the freedom of God's people grow. And may many new mango trees be the fruit of your ministry.

End Notes:

1. For a study on what Demons can do to Christians I recommend the book, *Demon Possession & the Christian. (Crossway Books, 1987)* C. Fred Dickason.

2. Other books for your consideration: C. Fred Dickason, *Demon Possession & the Christian;* Neil T. Anderson, *The Bondage Breaker*

3. C. Fred Dickason, *Demon Possession & the Christian;* Neil T. Anderson, *The Bondage Breaker*

4. Thayers definition

5. Names have been changed.

6. Neil T. Anderson, *The steps to FREEDOM IN CHRIST* (Gospel Light, Neil T. Anderson, 1990, 2001, 2004) Freedom In Christ Ministries, www.ficm.org

7. Dr. Ed Murphy, *The Handbook For Spiritual Warfare,* (Thomas Nelson Publishers, Inc.), P. 134.

8. Material taken from the teaching ministry of Oasis Ministries. Darren & Jennifer Rusco.

9. John Wimber.

Ministry Release Form

This is a pastoral ministry of deliverance and prayer. It is considered a form of biblical counseling, not professional counseling. I am not a licensed professional counselor. I work with you only as we choose to work together.

Both my associate and I commit to confidentiality in whatever you share with me. I am, however, required by law to report to appropriate persons two things:

1. Any intent of a person to take harmful, dangerous or criminal action against another person or against him or herself, or
2. Any act of child or elderly abuse or neglect.

If it appears that such notification needs to be given, it will be shared with you first.

In order to provide the appropriate legal protection, I ask that each person sign the following Statement of Release.

I Hereby release _____

and _____

from any liability should this ministry session not live up to my expectations or lead to any spiritual, emotional or physical dysfunction.

_____
Print Name

_____
Signed   Date

Made in the USA
San Bernardino, CA
01 May 2017